The Complete Handbook of Coaching Wide Receivers

The Difference Is the Details

S. "Chuck" Myers

ISBN-13: 978-1-58518-011-0
ISBN-10: 1-58518-011-4
Library of Congress Control Number: 2006939407
Cover design: Studio J Art & Design
Book layout: Bean Creek Studio
Front cover photo credits: Harry How/Getty Images

Coaches Choice
P.O. Box 1828
Monterey, CA 93942
www.coacheschoice.com

The Complete Handbook of Coaching Wide Receivers is a comprehensive, well-illustrated, and informative book that should be an integral part of every coach's library. In easy-to-understand detail, the book covers the skills and techniques of sound receiver play that can be utilized from youth football through the pros.

Charlie Stubbs
Assistant Head Coach/Offensive Coordinator
University of Tulsa

Coach Myers has a great grasp of the qualifications of a great receiver and how to develop those qualities. The drills and examples in the book are very valuable and have direct correlation to the game itself. The opportunity to become a better coach is in the pages of this book.

Doug Martin
Head Football Coach
Kent State University

As a former Consensus All-American and professional wide receiver, I found this book to be by far the best wide receiver coaching manual I have ever read. No stone was left unturned in the writing of this book. It is a very detailed and technically sound guide. All receivers coaches and players should benefit greatly from the use of this manual.

Jason H. Phillips
Wide Receivers Coach
University of Houston
Former All-American Wide Receiver

The Complete Handbook of Coaching Wide Receivers is an excellent resource for all coaches of all ages. It is thorough and extremely well-written. I was impressed with the depth of the book. Whoever reads this book, at whatever level they coach, will get something to take back to their team.

James Franklin
Offensive Coordinator
Kansas State University

As a former receiver and receivers coach, I found this book to be very informative. I have spent time with many Division I coaches and I think every idea and technique I have ever heard is included in this book. The research and knowledge put into it really shows.

Jim Collins
Head Football Coach
Capital University

As a former college All-American and NFL receiver, I found Coach Myers' book to be one of the best books that I have read about the wide receiver position. Coach Myers touches on every phase of the position and recommends great drills and coaching points for teaching the position.

Cedric Jones
Senior Director, Youth Football
National Football League

This book is a blueprint for how to coach the receiver position. If this reference guide had been available when I started coaching, I sure would have saved a lot of money on travel visiting other coaches.

Mike McCarty
Receivers Coach
Arkansas State University

The Complete Handbook of Coaching Wide Receivers is the most complete manual on wide receiver play I have ever read and should be used in every coaching theory class. Every coach should be this detailed in their position fundamentals and research.

Mike Santiago
Offensive Coordinator
Utah State University

Dedication

This book is dedicated:

- To my sweet daughter, Christina, the joy and the light of my life.

- To my oldest friend, Richard, who has always said, "Do what you really love to do, and all the rest will fall into place."

- To Jason Garrett, who was the first person I told I wanted to coach football and who from that time forward made me believe I could do it.

- To my Dad, who always encouraged us to reach for the stars and taught us how to dream.

- And especially to my beloved Mom, who has always taught me how to make those dreams come true—first when she was here, and now from above.

I have been blessed to be surrounded by wonderful people who have encouraged me and believed in me—no matter how improbable my football career might have seemed to them at the time. To all of these individuals, I am deeply grateful.

- Devin Bonik, then owner of the Emmitt Smith Football Camp and now assistant to the head coach for the Jacksonville Jaguars. Observing at his camps in the early years was inspiring. As I listened to so many stories of the obstacles Emmitt Smith and other pro players have overcome in trying to make their dreams come true, I began to believe I could learn to coach football without ever having played it. Years later as a coach at this camp, I felt I had arrived when Emmitt Smith stood quietly behind me as I was working with high school receivers and told me, "I like your drills."

- Duke Christian, who at the time was offensive coordinator at Southlake Carroll High School, Southlake, Texas. I called him out of the blue one day asking to serve as a volunteer at his football camp. I was a Harvard MBA with a decade of experience in investment banking in New York and Europe, but completely lacking in football coaching experience. Fortunately, he took me on for that camp and has always provided encouragement and wisdom.

- Fred Maples, then head coach of Southlake Carroll Middle School, who hired me as a "permanent substitute" coach (yes, that exists), which enabled me to spend a year learning the basics of football and the basics of coaching. I will forever be grateful to him for that and for the way he tried to "protect" me from other sports and other duties that kept impinging on my football time.

- Steve Brickey, now offensive coordinator and quarterbacks coach at Missouri State University, who gave me early opportunities to assist him in coaching at various football camps. My coaching skills in handoffs come from Coach Brickey.

- Darrell Dickey, head coach of the University of North Texas, Denton, Texas, who went way beyond the call of duty and opened wide the doors of the UNT football program to me. The two years I spent there were some of the best.

- Dante Wright, wide receivers coach of the University of North Texas in 1998, and his corps of receivers—who showed me how much fun it could be to coach wide receivers.

- Coach Clarence James, then the receivers coach (now running backs coach) at Southern Methodist University, who let me steal many great drills—including those that Emmitt Smith liked.

- Coach Joe Sawyer, defensive tackles coach at Southern Methodist University. Every time I work with Joe, I am reminded of the kind of coach I want to be. His knowledge, enthusiasm, and desire to always be learning, together with his ability to make others believe in themselves make him an especially inspiring coach to be around. To me he is the epitome of a coach.

- Ken Allen, a great coach to work for, and a friend who is there in the good times and even more "there" when the going gets rough.

- David Rascoe and Joe Breedlove, then head football coach and athletic director, respectively, at Fort Worth Country Day School, Fort Worth, Texas. They took a gamble and gave me my first high school coaching job.

Acknowledgments

- Coach James Hyden, formerly head coach at Sam Houston High School, Arlington, Texas, and athletic director of the Arlington Public Schools. He is a true inspiration as a coach and a person.

- The students, parents, and administration at the Oakridge School in Arlington, Texas provided encouragement and support, which meant so very much to me. Go Owls!

- Gary Oliver, then head coach at Bishop Lynch High School, Dallas, Texas, from whom I learned a lot and who led us with energy and wisdom through "that championship season."

- Todd Dodge, head coach of the 2005 Texas state champions and the mythical national champion Southlake Carroll Dragons, Southlake, Texas. Todd has supported me from early in my career, and gives me invaluable advice.

- Kevin Atkinson, currently head coach at Keller High School in Keller, Texas. He taught me the importance of "showing the love" to my players, an extremely important football and life lesson. Long live the Wildcats!

- Shae McCutchen, graduate assistant at the University of North Texas, who spent a hot Texas summer on the Astroturf and in the film room helping me take my game up a notch.

- Brill Garrett, a great friend and wise counselor, who patiently puts up with hours of dinner conversation about football—even when other topics might *occasionally* be more interesting.

- My football buddies, you guys know what you have done for me and what you mean to me: Hut Allred, Eric Anderson, Joel Berry, Chase Corley, Tom Engle, Kenny Evans, Scott Vestal, Todd Ford, Clayton George, Todd John, and Brad Shelly.

- Clint Bartel. I told you I wouldn't forget you when I wrote this book.

- Emily Robbins of the Dallas Cowboys, who has opened so many football doors for me, and, more importantly, who I am proud to call a friend for over 10 years now.

- Two great facilitators, H. Rexroat and Mac Miles—both with their own distinctive style. These two know how to work it.

- Barry Terranova, a great career counselor and agent who sees the myriad of synergies business skills can bring to a football program.

- Scott Agulnek and the Dallas Desperados of the Arena Football League, who made Desperados players and facilities available to us for the photo shoot for this book.

- Will Pettis, Jermaine Jones, and Jason Shelly, a special thank you to three great athletes who are fun and inspiring to work with. Go Desperados!

- Most of all "my" guys, those of you I have coached. No matter how hot the Texas day or how bitter the defeat, the times we've spent together on the turf have been the greatest. Always believe in yourselves—as I believe in you—and great things will happen. You have made it all worthwhile.

My favorite post-season award to give my football team is not MVP (Most Valuable Player) or Most Improved. My favorite award is the In the Trenches award. The person receiving the In the Trenches award is the person you would want in a foxhole with you during times of war. I think of this individual as courageous, energetic, loyal, somewhat feisty, and probably a tiny bit crazy. The four people who have worked with me on this book are my In-the-Trenches team: Maria Gomez, Janet McCready, Inger Miller, and Manny Trevino.

- Maria Gomez, who kept the book team fed and watered (if you knew us, you would realize what a huge job this is), and went way beyond the call of duty in lots of ways.

- Janet McCready—How lucky I am to live next door to a computer graphics genius. She never imagined, I am sure, how all-consuming this project would be when we started, but has stayed the course for a long number of months now.

- Inger Miller—How blessed I am to have a friend who is willing to spend many hours literally making sure the i's are dotted and the t's are crossed. She is not only a great grammarian, but her lively sense of humor has given us a lot of energy.

- And, most of all, Manny Trevino, whose various contributions to this book are too numerous to mention. More importantly, Manny has been an invaluable friend and supporter to me during my football career. Manny has been, and always will be, my go-to guy. How fortunate I am.

In the Trenches

Foreword

At Texas Tech, our offense is based on success in the passing game. Given that everything we try to accomplish offensively derives from that premise, we spend countless hours making certain that our receivers can get off the line of scrimmage, run precise routes with adjustments to get open, catch the ball, and gain yards after the catch. We also aggressively emphasize wide receiver blocking. In reviewing Coach Myers' book, *The Complete Handbook of Coaching Wide Receivers*, I have discovered a resource that will help my staff and me in our efforts to develop and improve our wide receivers' skills.

The most important skills our wide receivers learn are the correct fundamentals and techniques of the receiver position. We practice these essentials over and over again daily. Coach Myers' book concisely and clearly explains the principles of wide receiver play and provides instruction on how to develop receivers who will be successful on the field. Myers provides detailed diagrams and photos, as well as drills to reinforce the skill set being discussed.

The Complete Handbook of Coaching Wide Receivers is insightful, comprehensive, and a must-have resource for every coach who is serious about improving the efficiency of his passing game. Not only would I recommend this book for coaches—and players—from youth to the NFL, I will use it myself.

—Mike Leach
Head Football Coach
Texas Tech University

Contents

Several major factors combine to produce a successful wide receiver. Talent and a brilliant offensive system that showcases the receiver's abilities are obvious ones. However, it is technique that makes the difference between a good receiver and a great receiver. Technique is the foundation upon which success rests. The way to develop great technique is by paying attention to detail—knowing the specifics of what to coach receivers, and then observing your players with a keen eye to make sure that they are doing the "little things" correctly. As John Wooden says, "When you see a successful individual, a champion, you can be very sure that you are looking at an individual who pays great attention to the perfection of minor details."

This book is an in-depth study of receiver fundamentals. It is designed for high school coaches and college coaches new to the receiver position, and to serve as a reference tool for certain "controversial" issues that arise in coaching receivers. I have indicated my preferred method for teaching each technique, but I have also included a variety of viable ways a given technique may be taught—along with the pluses and minuses of each. Alternative methods are included so that each coach reading this book can select the one that makes the most sense to him given his own preferences, the age and skill level of his receivers, and the overall offensive package.

Drills relating to the topics discussed are included in each chapter, so that this manual may easily be used as a comprehensive teaching curriculum. Also, coaches who wish to locate "new" drills that address a particular aspect of the game should be able to do so easily.

I sincerely hope that this book will be useful to you, and that some of the knowledge gleaned here will help you produce receivers who have many magical moments on the turf.

> Note: In all photos in this book, the receivers are in white jerseys and the defenders are in dark jerseys.

STANCE AND START

Chapter One

The proper stance for a receiver is important because it enables him to get the maximum burst as he explodes off the line of scrimmage into his route. While a good stance and start do not guarantee a good route and great catch, they are the first steps (excuse the pun) in that direction. Things generally don't finish right if they don't start right.

Stance

Which Leg Forward?

The first issue that arises in coaching receivers is which leg should be forward in the stance. This section looks at each of these options:

- Inside leg up
- Outside leg up
- Multiple rules
- Receiver's choice

Inside Leg Up or "Outback"

A commonly used method is inside leg forward, outside leg back. This technique is the preferred method for two reasons:

- It gives all receivers a uniform look so that the defense cannot use the stance as a clue to ascertain which route is going to be run.
- If you are counting steps instead of yards to indicate the breakpoint on your routes, your receivers will be in a position to easily make the required break on the correct step and foot (e.g., the outside foot on a three-step slant).

Outside Leg Forward

The benefits of receivers placing the outside leg forward include:

- The receiver has slightly better vision inside to the football.
- It enables the receiver to go in motion more fluidly.
- It provides a faster takeoff for inside blocks (e.g., crack blocks) because the receiver's stance is more open to his target.

Multiple Rules

Some offenses (typically college-level) have multiple rules for which leg their receivers put forward in the stance. These rules are usually based on any or all of the following: the direction of the upcoming release, the route, the block, and whether the receiver is an outside receiver or a slot (inside) receiver. When the receiver factors in all these different components, these rules can create a high degree of complexity.

Receiver's Choice

Some offenses allow the receiver to pick which leg is forward. He may simply go with what is more natural and comfortable—which is usually to have the stronger push-off (jumping) leg forward. He also may choose to vary his stance based on his assignment on each play. A danger in this method is that a receiver may begin to tip off the direction of his route by, for example, starting with the inside leg up on a slant route and the outside leg up at all other times.

Correct Position in the Stance

In the preferred stance:

- The vertical distance between the front heel and the back heel is approximately the same as shoulder-width apart.

- The feet are hip-width apart.

- The shoulders are square to the line of scrimmage and over the front toes so that the receiver has forward body lean.

- The knees are slightly bent.

- The toes of both feet are pointed straight ahead, or the big toe of the forward foot may be slightly angled inside.

- The head and eyes are up.

- The arms are flexed with hands up.

These points describe a technically correct stance. However, slight adjustments should be made to make the receiver more comfortable in his stance, as well as when the defender is in press coverage (the defender jams the receiver at the line of scrimmage to disrupt his route, as discussed in Chapter 7).

Length of Stance

The length of the stance can be correctly attained in the following way. The receiver should stand with his feet parallel, shoulder-width apart, and straddling a yard line. He then raises the toes of the upfield foot and rotates that foot so that it points in a 90-degree angle upfield. Next, he raises the heel of the rear foot and turns it behind the toes of that foot. The receiver then slightly bends his knees and leans forward to put his shoulders over his front toes. With slight adjustments for comfort, the result is the perfect length for the stance. This stance is the preferred method because it minimizes false stepping (any extra foot movement that does not directly aid in takeoff) and it creates the most powerful takeoff possible.

The classic method for receivers has been an elongated stance with a large first step to gain ground. Taller receivers can gain a lot of depth with a longer stance, and they will feel comfortable in it. However, with most receivers, the coach needs to make sure that it is not "too much of a good thing" with the receiver exaggerating the length of his stance to the point of false stepping at takeoff. An overelongated stance is, in fact, one of the main causes of false stepping. The imbalance in weight distribution in an overelongated stance may also cause a slower takeoff from the line. Even at the college level, many receivers have stances that are too long for their body size.

Figure 1-1. Receiver position in the stance

Another method commonly used to position receivers in a stance is based on a track stance. The receiver takes a track stance (crouched over as if in starting blocks) and stands up from there. The receiver then has to adjust the length of his stance until it feels comfortable by either lengthening the stance or making it shorter. This is a "quick and dirty" way to get receivers lined up, but the coach must be sure to make individual adjustments.

Foot Position in the Stance

The preferred method for foot position in the stance is to have the upfield toe turned in at 11 o'clock when the right foot is forward and the upfield toe at one o'clock when the left foot is forward. This foot position gives more power to the initial step as the receiver pushes off over the big toe. This stance is generally a more natural and comfortable position than aligning with the front toe straight ahead (another acceptable method). What must not occur is for the front foot to point outside.

While some flexibility is allowed in the placement of the front foot, what is most important is that the back toe be pointed directly forward. Young receivers have the tendency to either pigeon-toe the back foot or more likely open it up (sometimes to a 90-degree angle) to help push off. This approach causes false stepping, slows down the takeoff, and potentially damages the knee.

For maximum acceleration on takeoff, the receiver should be on the balls of his feet with 80 percent of his weight on his front foot and 20 percent on his back foot or 90 percent and 10 percent depending on the strength of the receiver's stabilizer muscles. To ensure that his weight is sufficiently forward, a good test is to see if a piece of paper or a credit card can be slipped under the rear heel of the receiver—the heel should be at least that far off the ground.

Body Position in the Stance

After stance length and foot position are set, receivers need to have their knees slightly bent to be in ready athletic position in order to eliminate wasted motion as they start running. A common error is for young receivers to start too high and wait until the snap of the football to bend their knees and drop down to the correct takeoff position. Alternatively, they may start with their knees so flexed that the stance is awkward, and they are slow coming up from it to run. These errors require extra movement and waste time. To save time at takeoff, tell receivers to be in the correct position before the snap. They should be run-ready.

The receiver needs to also have forward body lean so that his chest is minimally exposed to a defender, who may be trying to jam him, and because this stance is the natural running position. Along with telling a receiver to put his shoulders over his toes, it is key to make sure the receiver's weight is distributed in such a way that he can power over his front leg at takeoff.

Arm Position in the Stance

While in the stance, a receiver may hold his arms in one of two positions:

- Bend the arms at the elbows and hold his hands chest high in front of his body with hands either relaxed or with clenched fists.

- Dangle the arms at his sides in a relaxed position.

The preferred method is hands held up in front of the body for three reasons:

- With his hands up at chest height, a receiver is ready to break a jam from a defender in press coverage. In fact, when a receiver's hands are higher than a defender's, he may be able to simply make a quick initial punch down on the defender's hands to help get a successful release (Chapter 4).

- The hands-up position gives the receiver a more powerful and threatening look. Since receivers are often considered contact-adverse, it is useful for them to look as aggressive as possible. (An intimidating stare by the receiver at the defender doesn't hurt either.) Also, this hand position works best with very young receivers who, if told to relax their arms at their sides, may relax too many other parts of their stance (and their minds) as well.

- In a natural running motion, the arms come up pumping forward and back. By starting with arms up, flexed, and run-ready, the receiver reduces the number of things he has to do for takeoff once the ball is snapped. One receiver has taken this point to the extreme: holding his arms as if he were already in running motion (i.e., right arm up and forward when the right leg is back in the stance). His left arm is cocked down and back. He begins the running motion from this position instead of having to maneuver his arms as he initiates it. At first this looks contrived, but he actually achieves a very strong and quick takeoff without wasted motion.

Closing the Stance Against Press Coverage

When faced with a defender in a press-coverage technique, a general rule is to have the receiver shorten the length of his stance. This position produces a tight, compact base and enables the receiver to initiate jab steps and takeoff steps quicker from the line. The quicker footwork is a key component in breaking the jam. It is also imperative for the receiver to keep his pad level low so that the defender has less surface area to attack. He should also have his arms flexed with his clenched fists held above the defender's hands and thus be ready to execute his hand release move.

Start

Coming to the Line

As the receiver runs (he never walks) to the line of scrimmage from the huddle, he needs to think about several things in addition to the correct stance:

- Aligning onside
- Checking his splits (alignment in relationship to the ball and other players) to make sure he is properly positioned on the field
- Scanning the defense and recognizing the coverage
- Developing a plan of attack for the release

Checking With the Line Judge

In games, the receiver should check with the line judge on his side on every play as he is aligning to make sure he is positioned correctly on or off the ball. The line judge will communicate and help. Checking with the line judge prevents penalties—especially at the middle and high school levels. Coaches need to instill this habit in practice and not just introduce the concept during the first game.

No part of the on-the-ball receiver's body can be in the neutral zone (length of the football). If it is, he may receive an offside penalty. The surest way for a receiver to be onside during a game is to line up on the line judge's foot, which this official uses to mark the line of scrimmage.

The off-the-ball receiver lines up off of the closest lineman's (tackle's or tight end's) rear-end. If the receiver is in the correct position, the line judge should be able to see space between that lineman's backside and the most forward part of the receiver (typically his head). To be safe, the off-the-ball receiver should also check with the line judge as he aligns.

Once the receiver is aligned correctly, he needs to make sure he does not receive an illegal motion penalty. Receivers can continue to move their hands after they are set, and they may need to in order to communicate information, such as route conversions, to the quarterback or coverage calls to other receivers. However, once they are set, if they move their feet at all or break the plane of the football with movements such as gesturing hands or moving heads, a penalty may be called.

Alignment on the Field

Depending on the offensive system and the preference of the head coach, alignment practices vary. Some general rules include:

- Outside receivers should line up using the numbers on the field as the point of reference. The horizontal position of the ball on the field and the designated route may determine whether to line up on the top, middle, or bottom of the numbers.

- The outside receiver should never align closer to the sideline than five or six yards.

- The slot receiver should split the distance between the closest lineman and the outside receiver.

- In a bunch formation, the three receivers are typically one yard apart with one of the receivers on the line of scrimmage.

- The receiver should consider the placement of the ball on the field. For example, if the ball is on the left hash mark, the wide receiver on the right side of the formation narrows his alignment (moves in toward the formation), and the wide receiver on the left side of the formation widens his alignment (moves toward the sideline).

- Receivers should evaluate before every play whether their splits need to be adjusted based on the type of route they are running. For example, a receiver who slightly narrows his splits (cheats in) for an out route has more room to execute this route.

- The strength of the quarterback's arm may play a role in the alignment of the wide receivers. If the quarterback does not have a strong arm, the receivers should not line up too wide.

- When a running play is called, unless otherwise specified, the receivers should take the maximum split in order to spread the defense horizontally.

Reading the Defense

The receiver needs to scan the defense and read the coverage (discussed in depth in Chapter 7). His reads include:

- Counting the number of safeties and checking their alignment

- Locating the linebackers and/or strong safety walked up (rover)

- Checking the cornerback's alignment and eyes

Often, young receivers tend to fix their eyes on the spot they plan to break at (or run to) and thus inadvertently give useful information to the defender. Therefore, a receiver should make these pre-snap reads in a systematic way each time he comes to the line. To make this habitual, tell the receiver to check the defense by scanning from safeties to linebackers to the cornerback on his side. If the receiver always makes his reads the same way when approaching the line of scrimmage, he will not tip off the defender as to where he is planning to go.

Release Plan of Attack

Players need to have a plan of attack for releasing off the line and running an effective route every time they come to the line (for more on these topics, see Chapters 4, 6, and 7). For now, recognize that receivers need to integrate the type of route they are running and the alignment of the defender covering them to decide pre-snap which side they will release to and which combination of hand and footwork is needed. Teach the receiver to attack the defender with a clear plan and not just to see what happens when he tries to release. This step is a key part of building a corps of aggressive and confident receivers.

At the Line

Stay Square

The receiver must stay square to the line of scrimmage (not tilting or tipping his body sideways even slightly); otherwise he may give away his release plan or route to a defender. Remind young receivers to keep their shoulders square and to turn their head—not their torso—to look inside for the snap of the ball.

At the Snap

The signal for the receiver to initiate his takeoff is the movement of the football at the snap. Going on ball movement instead of going on sound (the quarterback's cadence) minimizes offside penalties by your receivers. It also works consistently in large stadiums where crowd noise can be a problem when releasing on sound. Releasing only on ball movement is thus the preferred method, and drills should begin with a simulated snap to reinforce this point.

Takeoff

First Takeoff Step

The classic takeoff step is an extremely long step. Its purpose is for the receiver to gain as much ground as possible in one step. However, a shorter and more powerful drive step is the preferred method over a huge lunge forward for two reasons. Though less ground is gained on this initial step, this technique enables the receiver to get in the flow of his natural running motion faster. Also, the receiver maintains core strength to break the jam if it occurs. A good way to instill this technique is for a coach to hold the receiver's back heel while he is in the stance and takes his first step. This resistance ensures that the receiver makes the drive step strong, quick, and powerful.

It is important for the receiver not to pop up as he powers off the line, but rather to stay low and have forward body lean as he releases off the line of scrimmage. Doing so results in a faster takeoff. An Olympic sprinter does not stand straight up out of the blocks in the 100-meter dash. The same biomechanics apply for a receiver as he releases.

Running Technique During the Route

As the receiver runs, he needs to keep his arms pumping forward and back, close to his body, and to avoid any side-to-side swinging or swaying. In addition to running with forward body lean, he should run on the balls of his feet (running and speed drills are included in Appendix C). Also, he should have his eyes and head up to read the action and use peripheral vision and/or feel to locate the spot where he is going to make his break.

Keeping a low forward body lean throughout the route while gradually progressing up to proper running position is important because:

- It makes less body surface available for the defender to attack during press coverage.

- It helps convince the defender that the receiver is going deep on the route, which plays on his fear of getting burned for a touchdown and makes him bail.

- It enables the receiver to run faster and make his cuts quickly and more safely by promoting stability and balance.

Motion

A motion is when one offensive player aligned off the line of scrimmage moves from one spot to another before or during the snap. While that player is moving, all of the other offensive players must be set (still). A penalty—illegal motion—occurs when two players are in motion at the same time while the ball is snapped. Also, the motioning player must be moving parallel to (or away from) the line of scrimmage while the ball is snapped. If he is moving forward while the ball is snapped, it would be simulating the start of play, which is illegal. (In Arena Football, forward motion during the snap is allowed.) Motion may be used in an offensive scheme for several reasons:

- To help determine if the defense is in zone or man coverage. In man-to-man coverage, a defender typically shadows the receiver as he motions across the formation; in zone coverage, the affected defenders simply bump over a bit.

- To confuse the defense, who must adjust both their alignments and assignments on the fly as the cadence continues.

- To create a favorable mismatch with the defense. For example, the offense could motion to trips to overload half the field when the defense is in cover 2 (Chapter 10) or motion the best receiver to the area the weakest defender is covering.

- To loosen the defender off of the receiver, and gain a space and angle advantage in press coverage.

- To give a receiver a moving start on certain routes. For example, an outside receiver may motion inside to take off on a crossing route.

- To put a receiver in a better position for a block (e.g., a crack block), as well as to give him a running start on the block.

Types of Motion

Many variations in the use of motion can be implemented. Basic receiver motions include:

- Motioning inside toward the center of the formation

- Motioning all the way across the formation

- Motioning into the area behind the guard or tackle and back out to his original position

- Motioning from a tight alignment toward the sideline

- Motioning from outside to a wing position one yard outside of the tight end or to one yard inside the tight end (generally for blocking purposes)
- Motioning toward the running back in the backfield to set up a running play (like an end-around) or for blocking purposes

It is important to note the distinction between motion and shifting. A shift is a simultaneous change of position by two or more offensive players and can only happen before the snap. The shifting players must come to a stop and be set for at least one second before the ball is snapped.

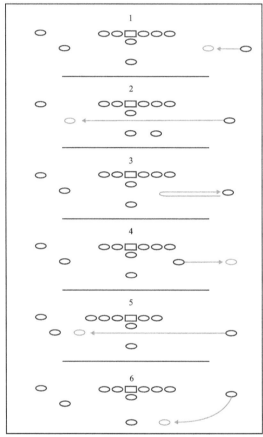

Figure 1-2. Selected motions made by the wide receiver

Drills

Stance and Start

Objective: To work on a proper stance and takeoff

Equipment Needed: One football

Setup: The players align along a yard line approximately three yards apart.

Execution: The receivers get in their stance. At the snap of the football (which the coach simulates), the receivers take off at approximately half-speed for 10 yards. The receivers

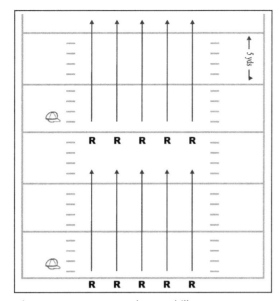

Figure 1-3. Stance and start drill

repeat this drill for several 10-yard intervals down the field while gradually increasing speed in each repetition until they are releasing and running the 10 yards at full speed.

Technique: The receiver releases on ball movement, powers off the line, and maintains low forward body lean. Make sure that each stance is correct, that the receivers are not making false steps as they release from the line, that they are driving off low and hard with their initial step, and that they are maintaining proper forward body lean throughout the drill.

Common Errors:

- Receivers use an incorrect stance.
- Receivers make the first step too large.
- Receivers false step.
- Receivers pop up as they take their initial step.
- Receivers look down instead of up.
- Receivers do not maintain forward body lean.

Things to Yell:

- "Shoulders over toes!"
- "Drive off the line!"
- "Stay low!"
- "Eyes up!"
- "Stay on balls of feet!"
- "I'm on your butt with a match!" (when you're chasing your receivers upfield)

Variation: To emphasize a powerful drive step off the line, the coach or an extra receiver holds the back heel in the stance as the receiver takes his first step.

Body Lean Takeoff

Objective: To improve the receiver's ability to burst off the line of scrimmage, and to maintain forward body lean as he runs

Equipment Needed: None

Setup: Align receivers three yards apart along a yard line.

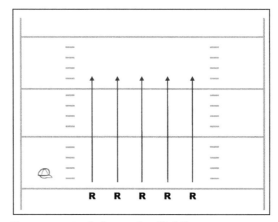

Figure 1-4. Body lean takeoff drill

Execution: Players stand on their tiptoes and lean as far forward as possible until they literally start to fall. As they fall forward, they start running. The falling-forward action ensures the receivers initially have correct forward body lean, which they must maintain throughout the 10 yards of the drill.

Technique: Receivers should use good forward body lean, run with their shoulders over their toes, and keep their eyes up.

Common Errors:

- Receivers pop up after two to three steps instead of gradually progressing up to the correct running position.
- Receivers look down as they run.

Things to Yell:
- "Low pad level!"
- "Don't pop up!"
- "Shoulders over toes!"
- "Eyes up!"

Variation: Have receivers start from the take-a-knee position with hands on the knee. Powering up from this position will also get them in the correct forward-body-lean position for the initial steps. Again, receivers must maintain proper body lean throughout the drill.

CATCHING
THE FOOTBALL

Chapter Two

All receivers have two jobs. One is blocking. Another is catching the football and scoring. While blocking is arguably the most important function of a receiver (since each receiver spends more time in games blocking than catching a football), receivers tend to be judged by their catching ability. This chapter discusses techniques of catching in general, as well as specific catching techniques based on the type of route being run.

Basic Catching: Hand Position

The basic rule of catching is to make a diamond-shaped window (some coaches teach a triangle) by putting the thumbs and index fingers of both hands together with the fingers spread out. This hand position is used when a football is coming waist high (belt buckle) or above, and directly to the receiver. When a ball is thrown below the waist, the hand position is the opposite: the pinkie fingers of both hands touch with thumbs pointing to the outside so that the hands form a basket to catch the ball. While common practice is to say waist high or above, the preferred method is to fine-tune the delineation point by using the bottom of the numbers, as the location that determines which hand position to use.

Figure 2-1. Window hand position

The Window: Big Eyes

The eyes are the most important component of the catch. Teach receivers to look through the window created by their hands. This technique is used not only to teach basic catching, but also to underscore the significance of using the eyes in the catch. Receivers should frame the incoming football with their hands and view the ball through the window. The receiver must maintain eye contact with the ball as it moves through the air, and he catches it—thus embracing the phrase "big eyes." Receivers should constantly practice catching the football with their eyes, hands, and the football all in the same frame.

Figure 2-2. Viewing the football through the frame

Focus and concentration are keys to getting the ball into the receiver's hands. Teach receivers to put "radar lock" on the ball, which means they lock their eyes on either the tip or the white stripe that forms a circle as the ball rotates in the air. The purpose of the small aiming point is if the receiver focuses on the whole football and he misses it, he misses it completely. If he aims at a smaller spot on the ball and misses that, it is still highly likely he will get his hands somewhere on the ball.

However, many passes will not be in front of the receiver, which makes him unable to view the ball through the frame. Other techniques—which are described later in this chapter—must be used for these types of catches.

Soft Hands and Big Hands

Teach receivers to catch with soft hands, which means to catch the ball with receptive fingers, wrists, and slightly bent elbows, and to give a little with the football as they catch it. Tai Chi, an ancient Chinese martial art, offers a useful lesson here. When two hard things collide with enough force, they often break. However, when a hard thing hits a soft thing, the softer thing can—by giving a little initially—control and manage the force. It is the same with catching a football—which can travel with a velocity of up to 70 miles per hour. The catch can be secured when the hands and elbows give and accommodate the force of the football. If the hands are too inflexible and hard, the ball will ricochet off.

Also, place emphasis on spreading the fingers apart during the catch. This use of big hands helps the receiver to cover more of the ball's surface area and in effect makes smaller hands bigger and the catch easier to secure. In fact, one of the key measurements an NFL scout looks for in receivers is the size of the hands. Of course, a receiver with smaller hands but proper technique can still be a great receiver.

Catch With the Fingers

Remind receivers to catch with their fingers and not the palms of their hands. One NFL receivers coach tells his players to snatch the ball from the air with their 10 fingers or 10 prongs—and not with their hands. Their fingers should be strong and powerful, slightly bent, and not stiff or straight. Receivers must grab the ball from the air with their fingers, and then cushion it with their palms while giving with the elbows.

A sign that a receiver is catching too deep in his hands is when an especially loud thud noise is heard when he makes the catch. In fact, if you look carefully at the hand action of receivers who are in a catching slump, you can often see that they are using their hands (palms) and not their fingers to initiate the catch.

Finger and hand exercises that build individual finger strength are extremely helpful. In addition to the typical grippers and squeeze balls, tools that work one finger at a time are especially useful. They not only improve mechanics, but also build the finger awareness that is crucial to catching (see the Special Equipment for Receiver Work section at the end of this chapter).

Arms Extended

Receivers need to catch the ball with their arms extended, and not with or against their bodies. If a ball in flight touches a receiver's body, it may ricochet off his shoulder pads making the pass incomplete—or worse. When his arms are extended and slightly bent, the receiver is able to use his elbows as shock absorbers to help cushion the catch as the ball makes contact with the hands.

Another reason to reach out with the arms to make the catch (and not wait for the ball to come into the body) is that the stretching out of the arms increases the distance between a defender who is behind the receiver and the football. If the receiver waits on the ball and then attempts to catch the ball against his body, the defender has a much greater chance of a deflection or an interception.

If the ball does pass through the receiver's hands (and he is lucky enough to trap it against his body), obviously the catch still counts. However, receivers must understand that a body catch is Plan B, and Plan A is to catch the ball in the hands with arms extended.

The Tuck

Once the receivers have caught the football, they must correctly tuck the ball to protect it from defenders. Tucking consists of watching the ball into the hands, and then locking it in a protected position using the hand, forearm, and elbow to squeeze the ball into the body. While coaches differ in the exact number of pressure points involved, it is imperative to have pressure from each of those three areas. Coach the receivers to run with the ball high and tight: high to maximize protection from tacklers, and tight against the body.

Coaches also disagree about how many fingers need to be held over the nose of the ball. Some programs teach one finger over the nose, and others teach two. The preferred method is two fingers, because two fingers give strong bilateral pressure.

The catch is not complete until the ball is tucked away. Receivers should tuck the ball every time they make a catch—even in the most basic warm-up drills in pre-practice. Demanding the tuck at all times instills discipline in your players, and adds crispness to your program. Tucking the football on every catch should become as automatic as breathing.

Figure 2-3. Tuck position

"The Eyes Have It" to the Tuck

The key coaching point on tucking the ball away relates to the eyes, and not to the hands. At any level of football, look at the number of passes that hit receivers' hands but get dropped—often because the receiver does not look the ball all the way into his hands. Instead, he looks up at the oncoming defender or starts to turn his body upfield to run too soon. Concentrating and watching the ball in until the tuck is complete will prevent many of these drops.

To drive home this point, make receivers call out, "Laces/no laces," depending on which side of the football is up whenever they catch a football. Some programs use this just in individual receiver drills, but others incorporate it throughout practice. One receiver made it such a habit that he shouted out the phrase as he made a touchdown reception in a game, and the cornerback thought he was trash-talking.

Different Kinds of Catches

This section analyzes the techniques used to catch balls thrown in different positions in relationship to the receiver. Teach receivers that if there is a problem with incomplete passes, they need to check their own technique and not blame the quarterback. This helps create a positive relationship between the quarterback and the receivers. The motto for receivers should be, "If it touches the skin, bring it in."

Balls in the Frame

Head-On Balls

These balls are ideally caught with the eyes looking through the window at the ball, arms extended in front of the chest, and the elbows slightly bent and with give in them.

While this basic catching position is useful for coaching technique, it rarely occurs in game situations. The reason for this is that this kind of catch only occurs when a ball is perfectly thrown on a couple of types of routes (e.g., stops and curls).

Crossfield Balls

When catching a ball on a crossfield route (i.e., dig, drag), the receiver needs to quickly get his eyes on the ball, get his hands around for the catch, and maintain his running stride. The receiver catches the ball with the correct hand position (diamond window facing the tip of the ball). Slight upper-body twisting will help get the correct angle on this catch.

High Balls

Among the several kinds of high balls are instances when the receiver is:

- Facing the quarterback (stop/curl)
- Moving continuously across the field perpendicular to the quarterback (dig/drag)
- Coming back to an underthrown deep ball (fade/corner/post)

Facing the Quarterback (Stop/Curl)

When a ball is thrown directly at a receiver, but up high, he needs to place his hands high and in front of his body. As he makes the catch, he should see the ball move all the way into his hands. Receivers tend to wait to catch this ball until it is almost directly over their heads. They then lose sight of the ball at the last second. If a receiver cannot catch the ball high and in front where he can see it, he needs to tilt his head back so that he keeps the football in sight at all times. This type of catch is, of course, not the easiest thing to do in shoulder pads and a helmet. Hence, catching high and in front should be repeatedly drilled. It is a reaction issue, and the reflexes need to be quick.

Figure 2-4. High-ball catch on a stop route

Encourage receivers to stay on the ground unless it is absolutely necessary to jump for the catch. Jumping is a bad habit some develop to enable them to secure catches easier by cradling the ball into their body instead of reaching out to it with their hands. Be sure to remind receivers not to leave the ground unless the ball is so overthrown that they must jump to make the catch.

When they must truly go airborne to get their hands on the ball, receivers need to time and position their jump with the hand/eye mechanics previously discussed. In other words, they must always see what they catch.

Moving Continuously Across the Field (Dig/Drag)

When catching a high ball on a crossfield route (dig, drag), the receiver needs to keep his eyes on the ball, keep his head up, get his hands in the diamond position and around for the catch, and maintain his running stride. Again, the receiver should not jump for the ball unless it's unreachable from the ground. This technique is especially important on these types of routes as the receiver has great running momentum going already.

Figure 2-5. High-ball catch running crossfield

If the ball is thrown high and so far in front of the receiver's path that he must extend his upper body way out (or even lay out airborne for the ball), conventional practice is for the receiver to use the diamond window hand position to make the catch. If a receiver does this well instinctively, it is great. However, you may notice a lot of drops on this type of catch for the following reasons:

- The receiver does not get his hands sufficiently around, and the ball hits the sides of his hands.
- The receiver's hands come at the ball too high and bat it down.
- As the receiver lands, the football is less secure upon contact with the ground.

Therefore, the pinkies-together hand position is the preferred method because it enables the receiver to make an easier catch that is less likely to be dropped.

However, if the ball is so far from the receiver's body that it is virtually unreachable, an alternative is for the receiver to use the thumbs-together-and-hands-around technique. The biomechanics are sometimes such that, for the virtually uncatchable ball, this hand position provides the arms the greatest extension, and allows extra momentum for laying out for the ball.

Underthrown Deep Ball (Fade/Corner/Post)

Strangely enough, a receiver must turn an underthrown deep ball into a high ball. When the receiver recognizes that a deep ball is underthrown, he stops his progression by planting his upfield foot and turning around to change direction to come back toward the football. He then needs to "high-point" the football by jumping to catch the ball at its highest point so the defender cannot get to it. When jump balls of this sort do occur, the receiver must have ultimate concentration and have his eyes completely fixed on the football. If a receiver is working one-on-one against a defender, remind him to use his body to shield the ball from the defender. This technique is similar to a basketball player blocking out and going up to get a rebound.

Figure 2-6. High-point catch

At times, the ball may be so badly underthrown that the defender is in a better position to make the catch than the receiver is. In this situation, the receiver becomes the defender. When he cannot secure the catch himself, he may need to aggressively deflect the pass in order to prevent the defender from intercepting it. Sometimes the receiver might purposely commit an offensive pass interference penalty to ensure that the defender does not make the catch.

Low Balls

When a ball is thrown head-on and low to a receiver, he needs to bend his knees and get low. He absolutely must bend from the knees and not the waist. Receivers tend to underestimate how much they need to bend their knees (it's uncomfortable) to be able to get under the ball. Therefore, the key on all low balls is, "Go lower than you think you need to go."

The receiver then scoops the ball up (hand position is pinkie finger to pinkie finger with big hands) to make sure the ball does not touch the ground. Watch your receivers carefully and you will see that low catches are often missed because the receivers do not get their hands quite low enough and end up knocking the ball down. Instead of scooping the ball up, they actually bat the ball down.

Figure 2-7. Head-on low ball catch

When the ball is thrown low and to the side of a receiver, he needs to adjust to the ball by aligning himself directly in front of the path of the ball. Catching low balls with the hands out to the side has a very low success rate. Therefore, only as a last resort should a receiver try to catch this type of low ball without first aligning himself directly in front of it.

Occasionally, a ball is thrown low and so far to the side that the receiver has to lay out for it. When he does, the receiver should have his arms and elbows extended with palms up, and pinkies together. Laying out and using the pinkies-together hand position enables him to get his hands under the ball and scoop it up, and thus minimizes the risk of inadvertently batting it down. When the catch is made, he should simultaneously turn to his side as he hits the ground if at all possible. This protects the receiver from getting the breath knocked out of him. It also creates a natural barrier between the ball and the ground and gives the receiver a second chance to secure the catch if he does not have a firm grip on it. Laying out for the ball is difficult and somewhat dangerous to drill, but the concept should be introduced early on (a basic drill that minimizes injury risk is included at the end of this chapter).

Often, referees do not have a clear visual on whether a very low ball is truly caught or just trapped by the receiver's body. Therefore, the receiver should immediately, while still on the ground, hold the ball up to demonstrate that he has control of it. Doing so helps show everyone—especially the officials—that he has truly made the catch. Some might even suggest that the receiver do this when he has just trapped the ball, as well as when he has actually caught it.

Figure 2-8. Laying out for a low ball

Balls Thrown Behind the Receiver

Quarterback coaches spend a lot of time telling quarterbacks to lead the receiver when throwing the football. However, balls are often thrown slightly behind the receiver in such a way that he has to open and turn the hips—flip the hips—to get his upper body turned, and to get his hands back around to catch the ball. Hand position in this catch follows the regular high- and low-ball rules. This catch is difficult to make, but one that occurs fairly often and must be drilled frequently. It should be included in the receiver warm-up drills at practice and before games. It is important to get those hips open and flipping.

Figure 2-9. Flipping hips on a ball thrown behind the receiver

Some offenses include a pass purposely thrown to the hip of the receiver on routes such as a fade route versus man-to-man coverage (Chapter 7). Since the defender is in a full sprint with his eyes focused on the receiver, he does not see the ball coming. Therefore, the receiver can quickly get his hands around and snag the ball before the defender can throttle down to reverse his upfield momentum and go after the ball.

Over-the-Shoulder Balls

To catch an over-the-shoulder ball on routes such as the post, corner, and fade, the hand position is pinkie fingers together and palms up. The receiver's eyes must follow the trajectory of the ball over his shoulder and into his hands. The receiver brings the ball straight into his body, cradling it as he moves it to the tuck position.

A key coaching point here is to ensure that the receiver only puts his hands up for the catch at the last second. The reason for this delay is so the defender—who at this point typically has his back to the ball—has the minimum amount of time to realize the receiver is about to catch the ball, thus reducing his ability to make a play. Also, when a receiver runs with his hands out, it slows down his speed, and increases the chances of an overthrown ball.

Adjusting to Off-Target Balls

A receiver may run deep while looking for a pass over his inside shoulder, only to realize the pass will come over his outside shoulder. An example is a deep-post ball that the quarterback overthrows to the outside instead of leading the receiver toward the middle of the field. The receiver must immediately recognize how to adjust his path to catch the football.

If the ball is slightly off the correct path, the receiver can simply adjust the angle of his route and make the catch as planned over his inside shoulder. This technique is called "adjusting to the ball."

If the ball is dramatically off-target, another type of adjustment must be made. This play is a low-percentage play, but it can result in a spectacular catch when it works. Look at it as a lemons-to-lemonade scenario. The receiver must change the direction of his route by turning his back to the football in flight and running to the splashdown area where he will catch the ball over his other shoulder. The receiver should execute the turn as quickly as possible and get his head around immediately to find the football with his eyes.

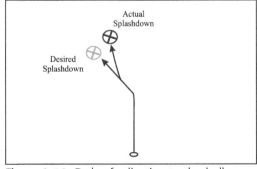

Figure 2-10. Path of adjusting to the ball

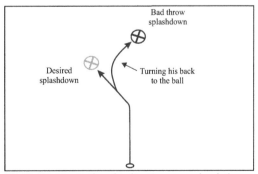

Figure 2-11. Path of adjusting to a bad throw over the wrong shoulder

Sideline Balls

Often a receiver will have to make a catch as he is barreling toward the sideline or the back of the end zone. At this point, the receiver must show that he has control of the ball, and make the catch with one foot inbounds (both feet in the NFL). He cannot be juggling the ball as his momentum takes him out of bounds. Receivers need to develop a feel for the boundary, and throttle down soon enough to stay inbounds for the catch. Besides thinking about shortening their stride dramatically by chopping their feet, receivers can practice tiptoeing toward the sideline. Rising up on their toes in a tiptoe motion automatically cuts stride length. Drills, like the ones in this book, must be practiced for the footwork and to develop a feel for the location of the line. It is important to practice this type of catch because receivers initially tend to look at their feet and the line instead of staying focused on the catch.

Also, when a ball is thrown far enough that the receiver has to stretch out to catch the ball, the receiver must execute a toe drag in order to stay inbounds. The toe drag is the final action that lets the receiver stay inbounds while enabling him to extend the upper body as far as possible out of bounds to secure the catch. Again, make sure that the receiver practices the toe drag enough that he can automatically execute it in a game situation while focusing on making the catch.

Figure 2-12. Sideline catch

Two-Handed Versus One-Handed Catches

The preferred method is that players should be told to catch the ball with two hands. If players are allowed to make one-handed snags in practice, it may come back to haunt you in a game. If a receiver reaches out for the ball with one hand and misses it, he misses it. If he has both hands extended, he may end up tapping it with one hand into the other by using the second hand almost like a baseball mitt (it is interesting to note that back in the day, receivers were expressly taught to make catches in this fashion).

One-handed catching drills do develop heightened finger and hand dexterity. And, if you can catch routinely with only one hand, how much easier it is then to catch with both hands. However, finger and hand dexterity can be as effectively developed in a number of other ways (see hand exercises in Appendix C). When practicing live catching, drills should simulate game situations as much as possible, and one-handed catches in games are not what should be coached. Of course, if it happens in a game, the receivers coach will be as happy as anyone.

However, at college level and above, one-handed catching drills make sense because basic catching skills are already well-cemented. Also, the great sophistication of the defenders at this level, and the "let them play" mentality of the refs, mean receivers may literally have to make catches with one hand tied behind their backs.

Drills

Partner Passing

Objective: To work on basic catching and tucking techniques

Equipment Needed: One football for every pair of receivers

Setup: Have the receivers pair up and face their partners at a distance of five yards. The receivers in one line have the footballs.

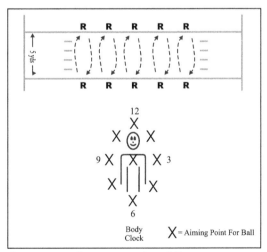

Figure 2-13. Partner passing drill

Execution: The receiver throws the football to his partner in the line facing him. The velocity of the throw steadily increases during the drill. First, the receiver catches the ball with his hands out in front of his body as the ball is thrown to the middle of his chest. He makes a laces/no laces call as he tucks the ball away. Next, he catches balls in several positions (with his arms moving around his body like the hands of a clock), as follows:

- High over his head (12 o'clock)
- High and outside to the left (1 o'clock)
- To the left (3 o'clock)
- Low and outside to the left (4 o'clock)
- Low (6 o'clock)
- Low and outside to the right (8 o'clock)
- To the right (9 o'clock)
- High and outside to the right (11 o'clock)

At this point, one line turns their backs to the first group. Each receiver throws the ball over his partner's shoulder to simulate the fade ball. During all of this drill, the coach should walk up and down the line of receivers correcting their technique, making sure they are making the right laces/no laces call, punching the ball out of their hands when they have weak tucks, and so forth.

Technique: The receiver finds the ball with his eyes by looking through the diamond window when possible. He catches the ball in his fingers with his hands out in front of his body, arms slightly bent, and his eyes always on the ball. He looks the ball all the way into his hands and into the correct tuck position with two fingers over the nose.

Common Errors:

- Receivers catch the ball with their bodies and not in their hands.
- Receivers catch with the palms of their hands instead of in their fingers.
- Receivers are inconsistent in their tucks and their laces/no laces calls.
- Receivers take their eyes off the football.

Things to Yell:

- "Keep your eyes on the ball!"
- "Catch in your fingers!"
- "Ten prongs!"
- "Big hands!"
- "Soft hands!"
- "Tuck the ball away!"
- "Give me a laces/no laces call!"
- "You're not looking it all the way in!"

Variations:

- The drill can progress from the initial 5 yards, to 10, and then to 15 yards.
- To help receivers improve reaction time, have them start with hands behind their backs and only bring them up when the ball is released.
- If the receivers start to feel whether the laces are up or down, as opposed to looking the ball all the way in (and they will), it is useful to mark numbers with

a Sharpie on the nose of each quadrant of the football. Then, since no crime goes unpunished, make the receivers call out the number that is up as they tuck the ball instead of making the laces/no laces call.

Hands Around the Goalpost

Objective: To ensure that the receivers catch the ball in their fingers with their hands extended away from their bodies and with give in the elbows

Equipment Needed: Three footballs and one goalpost

Setup: The first receiver stands up against the goalpost facing the coach, who is 10 yards away. He gets into good football catching position and pumps his arms (simulating a running motion) while waiting for the throw.

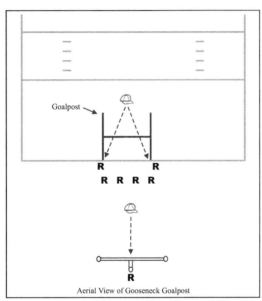

Figure 2-14. Hands around goalpost drill

Execution: The receiver catches the ball in his fingers with his arms extended around the goalpost. The goalpost ensures the receiver cannot catch the ball against his body.

Technique: The receiver should catch the ball in his fingers with his arms extended away from his body. His arms and hands give during the catch. He quickly locks the ball away in the correct tuck position.

Common Errors:

* Receivers catch the ball in the palms of their hands and not with the fingers.
* Receivers do not take the time to tuck the ball away.

Things to Yell:

* "Keep your eyes on the ball!"
* "Keep your elbows flexed!"
* "Catch in your fingers!"
* "Big hands!"

- "Soft hands!"
- "Look it in!"
- "Tuck it!"

Variation: Once the receivers have mastered this drill, it is useful to have one or two receivers stand beside and slightly in front of the receiver who is catching the ball. Have them distract the receiver by waving their arms and coming as close to deflecting or intercepting the ball without actually touching it as they can. This drill is a very close-in and intense distraction drill and it's something your receivers can have fun with. You may even get some pseudo-trash-talking (boasting, teasing), which will liven up practice for them.

Warm-Up Catching Drills

Objective: To get receivers loose and focused on the different techniques used to catch basic types of passes. This drill is a good early practice and pre-game drill because a lot of catches are made and not much running is required.

Equipment Needed: Two footballs

Setup: Line up the receivers single file on a yard line across the field. Initially, the coach stands 10 yards in front of and 10 yards perpendicular to the receivers.

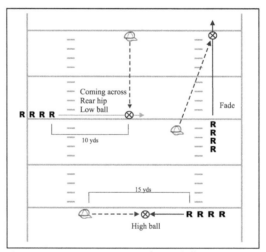

Figure 2-15. Warm-up catching drill

Execution:

- Coming across—Each receiver jogs along a yard line and catches a pass thrown chest-high in front of him. When all receivers have gotten their rep, the receivers reverse the drill, and come back across from the opposite direction (same type of pass).
- Rear hip—The receiver jogs across the same yard line, but the coach aims the ball at the rear hip of the receiver (a pass that is all too common in a game situation). The receiver must flip his hips—not just put his hands around—in order to catch the ball. The receivers then repeat by coming back from the opposite direction.

- Low ball—The coach pitches a low ball to each receiver as he comes across the field. This drill is great for getting the knees bent, and to reinforce scooping the ball up from low to high with both hands instead of batting at it from above. Again, repeat from the opposite direction.
- High ball—The receivers line up facing the coach at a depth of approximately 15 yards. They jog forward, are thrown a high ball, and go up and catch it at its highest point.
- Fade—The receivers line up parallel to the coach and jog about 7 to 10 yards down the field as the coach throws a fade ball.

Technique:

- Coming across—Does the receiver use the correct hand position (diamond)? Does he catch with his fingers and eyes and tuck the ball away?
- Rear hip—Are hips opened and flipping? Does the receiver quickly turn his head and get his hands in the correct position?
- Low ball—Does he bend from the knees and not the waist? Is the receiver "going lower than he thinks he needs to go?" Does the receiver use the correct hand position (pinkies together)?
- High ball—Is the receiver high-pointing the ball? Are both the hands and the ball in the line of sight as he makes the catch?
- Fade—Is he adjusting properly to the ball? Is the receiver staying in full running motion as long as possible and sticking his hands up just before the ball reaches a catchable point? Does the receiver use the correct hand position (pinkies together)?

Common Errors:

- Coming across—Receivers have incorrect hand position.
- Rear hip—Receivers don't flip the hips, just the hands.
- Low ball—Receivers do not bend their knees low enough.
- High ball—Receivers wait to catch the ball until the ball is directly overhead instead of going after the ball and catching it when they can still see it.
- Fade—Receivers lose sight of the ball. Also, they do not adjust properly to the flight of the ball.

Things to Yell:

- "Look it in!"
- "Flip the hips!"
- "Go lower than you think you need to go!"
- "High-point it!"
- "Adjust to the ball!"
- "See what you catch!"

- "Tuck the football!"
- "Great catch!" (especially when you have put a ball in a very hard-to-reach position, either on purpose or inadvertently)

Pat-and-Go

Objective: To work on catching the football and staying on the stem (vertical path from takeoff to the breakpoint) of a route. This drill is a good warm-up for both quarterbacks and receivers.

Equipment Needed: Four footballs

Setup: Two lines of receivers are lined up diagonally and crossfield on yard lines with a quarterback throwing to each line. Each line of receivers is in on a yard line adjacent to and 10 yards away from each quarterback. The quarterbacks are diagonally 20 yards from each other.

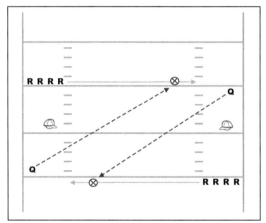

Figure 2-16. Pat-and-go drill

Execution: Routes that can be run during this drill include the stop, curl, fade, and go, and they should be run in order from shortest to longest. The quarterback simulates the snap by patting the ball. The receiver releases and runs along a yard line, which works on the receiver's ability to stay on the vertical stem of a route and alerts him if he strays from it. The receiver runs the designated route, catches the ball, and secures the tuck. After the ball is caught, the receiver finishes his run and hands the ball to the quarterback on the same side where he just finished the route and joins that line of receivers. The quarterbacks and receivers can widen from the initial 10-yard distance after the quarterbacks' arms begin to get warm and loose.

Technique: The receiver must start from a correct stance, run the route staying on the stem, and catch the football using proper hand technique.

Common Errors:

- The receiver does not burst off the line, run with good form, or stay on the stem (yard line).
- The receiver does not catch the ball, even though the drill should be a relatively routine throw and catch on air (no defenders).

- The receiver does not use proper hand technique in catching the ball.
- The receiver does not tuck the ball after the catch.

Things to Yell:

- "Eyes on the football!"
- "Adjust to the ball!"
- "Big hands!"
- "Soft hands!"
- "Look it in!"
- "Tuck the ball!"

Diving Catch

Objective: To work on the receiver's ability to make a diving catch (minimizing the risk of injury).

Equipment Needed: Two footballs

Setup: The first receiver gets on his knees 10 yards from the coach.

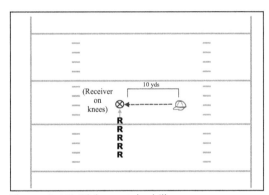

Figure 2-17. Diving catch drill

Execution: The coach throws the ball one to two yards in front of and to the side of the receiver in such a way that he must lay out to catch the ball.

Technique: The receiver dives out to catch the ball. Arms and elbows are extended, with palms up, pinkies together, and the hands under the football. The receiver scoops the football into his body, rolls on his side, and secures the ball as in a fumble-recovery drill. He then holds the ball in the air to show the official he has made the catch.

Common Errors:

- The receiver scoops the ball from a bent-knee position without laying out flat.
- The receiver does not move quickly enough to protect the football.
- The receiver does not sell the catch.

Things to Yell:

- "Lay out flat!"

- "Keep your hands together!"
- "Protect the football!"
- "Show me you caught the ball!"

Variations:

- This drill may also be done as a partner passing drill.
- This drill minimizes injury risk, but does not let the receiver get the full feeling of laying out flat. You can fix that limitation if you have access to pole-vault mats. Have the receiver jog toward the mat. The ball should be thrown in the middle of the mat so the receiver has to dive to make the catch. Doing so gives him the experience of going airborne while fully unlocking his hips and laying out flat.

Reaction Drill

Objective: To improve the receiver's ability to react quickly to the flight of the football

Equipment Needed: Two footballs

Setup: The receiver is 10 yards from the coach, and has his back turned toward him.

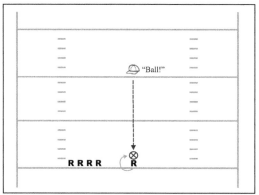

Figure 2-18. Reaction drill

Execution: The coach releases the ball while shouting, "Ball!" The receiver quickly turns around, catches the football, and tucks it away. The first time through, the receivers turn to the right, and the second time they turn to the left.

Technique: The receiver should quickly get his feet and body turned 180 degrees in one motion. The initial phase of this motion is to vigorously pull the elbow in the direction he is turning to create momentum for the rest of the body to follow. The receiver must immediately find the ball with his eyes and quickly get his hands in the correct catching position.

Common Errors:

- The receiver does not get his head and body around fast enough.
- The receiver does not locate the ball in the air quickly enough to catch it.
- The receiver catches the ball against his body and not with his fingers.

- The receiver does not tuck the ball quickly and/or does not use his eyes to look it all the way in.

Things to Yell:

- "Throw your elbow!"
- "Get your head around!"
- "Eyes up!"
- "Find the football!"
- "Catch in the fingers!"
- "Look it in!"
- "Tuck the ball away!"

Variations:

- Have the receiver lie flat on his back with his feet in the direction of the coach. When the coach yells, "Ball," he pops up and finds the football.
- To increase complexity, you can have the receiver initially lie with his head in the direction of the coach.

Sideline Drill

Objective: To teach receivers to catch a ball inbounds when the throw is on the sideline and almost out of bounds

Equipment Needed: Three footballs

Setup: Line the receivers up 10 yards from the sideline along a yard line. The coach stands five yards perpendicular to and midway between the receivers and the sideline.

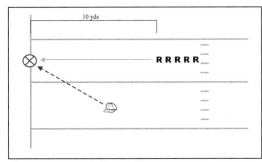

Figure 2-19. Sideline drill

Execution: The receiver runs full speed toward the sideline to simulate the top of an out route. The coach throws him a pass so that the ball arrives when the receiver is right at the sideline. The receiver must catch and show control of the ball with one foot inbounds. A great catch isn't a catch if the receiver is out of bounds.

Technique: The receiver must be aware of where the sideline is, know when he needs to throttle down his running motion into choppy little steps and tiptoe, and if/when to execute the toe drag. If the receiver has any room to turn and run upfield after the catch, he must do so.

Common Errors:

- The receiver will not begin his throttle-down action soon enough, and will catch the ball out of bounds.
- The receiver will not have control of the ball in the catch.

Things to Yell:

- "Chop now!"
- "Tiny feet!"
- "Toe drag!"
- "Catch it first!"

It is not so much *what* to yell here as to be able to judge *when* to yell. A novice receiver needs help knowing when to start throttling down in order to catch the ball inbounds. The trick is for him to start tiptoeing soon enough but not any earlier than necessary, or he will not gain maximum separation from the defender who is trailing him. The coach may therefore need to shout, "Chop" when the receiver should begin to throttle down.

Variation: A variation is the end-zone catch. The coach stands on the 10-yard line and throws each receiver a vertical or fade ball as the receiver approaches the end line. The receiver must secure the catch—and be in control of the football—while throttling down enough to keep one foot inbounds in order to have the touchdown be valid.

Distraction Drill

Objective: To improve the receiver's ability to catch a football in traffic

Equipment Needed: Three footballs

Setup: Receivers line up on a yard line facing a line of distracters who are 15 yards away. The coach is in the middle and 10 yards away from the yard line.

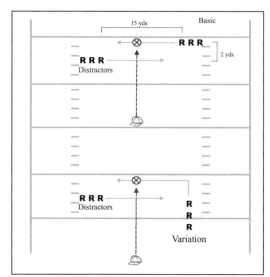

Figure 2-20. Distraction drill

Execution: At the snap, the receiver takes off on a crossfield path at the same time as the defender releases on a similar crossfield path two yards in front of him. It is important that they time their pace to meet in the middle of the drill. At the point where the paths of the two players cross, the defender waves his arms over his head, jumps, shouts, or does anything else he can think of to distract the receiver from catching the pass. The defender can do anything short of touching the ball.

Technique: The receiver must keep his eyes glued on the football and maintain a high level of concentration throughout the drill in order to make the catch.

Common Errors:

- The receiver loses sight of the football, and does not catch it.
- The ball hits the receiver's hands, but he does not secure the catch and tuck.

Things to Yell:

- "Keep your eyes on the ball!"
- "Concentrate, focus!"
- "White stripe, tip of the ball!" (to remind receivers to radar lock on the ball)
- "Soft hands!"
- "Tuck it!"

Variations:

- Receivers do not have to just come straight across the field. The receiver may simulate the tops of various kinds of routes (e.g., a square-in), while the defender simply continues to run on his crossfield path. Doing so enables the receivers to work on correct footwork in the break as well as to locate the ball and secure the catch through the arms of a defender. A further variation has the defenders mirroring the same routes instead of just coming straight across the field. Doing so gives the defenders an opportunity to work their breaks as well and makes practice time more efficient.
- Stationary reaction/distraction drill: The receiver lines up with his back to the coach. A defender is two yards in front of the receiver. The coach yells, "Ball" as he releases the pass. As in the previous example, the defender distracts the receiver who must turn quickly around and catch the football.

Trampoline Drill

Objective: To improve the receiver's ability to make acrobatic catches by having him catch the football in various contorted positions with minimal risk of injury as he falls. This drill will probably take place off-site and outside of regular practice hours. General trampoline safety rules must be enforced.

Equipment Needed: Two footballs and a trampoline

Setup: A receiver stands on a trampoline. The coach is on the ground and 10 yards away from the trampoline.

Execution: The receiver jumps on the trampoline. The coach throws the ball at several different aiming points to make the receiver vary the adjustments he has to make in order to catch the football. The receiver catches the ball airborne while using whatever body position is necessary to make the catch.

Technique: The receiver must adjust to the football in flight and make an airborne catch with the correct hand position. To make this drill realistic and useful, the receiver must remain in good football position as much as possible and use moves that can be transferred to game situations.

Common Errors:

- Receivers lose sight of the football.
- Receivers catch the football with the wrong hand position or against their bodies.

Things to Yell:

- "Stay in control!"
- "Keep your eyes on the ball!"
- "Lay out!"
- "Go get it!"
- "Stay with it!"
- "Watch the ball all the way in!"

Variations:

- The trampoline can also be used to work on diving catches. In this case, the receiver stands at one end of the trampoline. The coach throws the ball to the area over the middle of the trampoline where the receiver makes a diving catch.
- The trampoline may be used for "find the football" drills. The receiver starts jumping with his back to the ball. The ball is thrown on a ball call. The receiver turns around, locates the ball in flight, and makes the catch while laying out if necessary.

Special Equipment for Receiver Work

Gripmaster

The Gripmaster is not the classic squeeze ball or V-shaped "gripper," although those are useful, too. Rather, the Gripmaster is a tool that exercises each finger individually. It strengthens fingers, hands, and even forearms. Catching problems often exist because the receiver is palming the ball, and this equipment strengthens fingers so they can play a bigger role in catching. It also helps psychologically as it builds awareness of the fingers (not just hands) as a key to catching.

The Gripmaster offers a placebo effect as well. When a receiver is in a slump, buy him one as a gift, and tell him it has worked magic for other guys whose catching has suddenly gone bad. In so many cases, receivers have improved quickly and dramatically once they started using this tiny piece of equipment. It has brought more than one Texas State Champion football player out of a catching slump. Gripmasters can be found at www.gripmaster.net.

Bungee Balls

Plastic bungee balls can be hooked on any chain link fence, and are outstanding for improving hand-eye coordination, speed of reflexes, and catching with the fingers. Because no running is involved, bungee balls are a great and safe way to make use of pre-practice and other waiting-around time, and receivers can make hundreds of catches in a short amount of time. Bungee balls can be found on the Internet at www.worldsportinggoods.com.

Net Drills

Most catching drills can be done in front of a net. The advantage is that much less time is spent chasing loose footballs. A moderately sized soccer goal frame (as small as 12 x 6 feet) may be used. Alternatively, the frame can be easily built from PVC pipe if the soccer team cannot spare an old frame. The two ends of the goal should either have a solid base or alternatively large stakes at the bottom so that the net can easily be driven into the ground when it is moved from one location to another. If you use one of these nets, you will find you can get a lot more catching reps executed in a shorter period of time. It will add significantly to the crispness of your individual practice time.

Jugs

As with net drills, most throwing drills can be done with a Jugs machine. A Jugs football throwing machine is expensive (approximately $2000), but very useful for a school's receiver corps because:

- The machine may be set so that balls come at a variety of different angles and speeds (up to 100 miles per hour). The Jugs machine is also very useful for working punt and kickoff return.

- A high number of repetitions can be performed in a relatively short time because the machine spews out up to 600 balls in one hour.

- Ends of routes and catches can be worked efficiently without the receiver overtiring his legs by running long distances (also true for end-of-route work with balls thrown the old-fashioned way).

These machines can be found at numerous places including www.thejugscompany.com.

GreatCatch

GreatCatch hand straps are small elastic bands with mini tennis balls connected to them. The receiver puts the band around his hands, with the balls in the palms. While wearing the GreatCatch hand straps, the receiver must catch the ball with his fingertips. If he tries to catch the football with his palms, it will bounce off the mini tennis balls and he will not make the catch. The straps come with different sizes of mini tennis balls so they work for receivers with big or small hands. GreatCatch hand straps are excellent tools for learning to catch with the fingers and with soft hands. They can be found at www.greatcatch.org.

PASS ROUTES

Chapter Three

An infinite number of routes and route packages are possible. This chapter analyzes each of the fundamental route types. Knowing proper technique for these individual routes means that the receiver is ready for any combination of routes—no matter how bizarre—that the head coach might conjure up in the middle of the night. The chapter starts with a few general comments on routes. In-depth descriptions of basic routes, hybrid routes, screen routes, goal-line routes, and pick routes follow.

General Comments

Deception and "Selling Deep"

To be a good wide receiver, a player needs to be good at deception. A key element in the deception process is to make the defender think the receiver is running a different route than he actually is by selling another route. Deception starts as the receiver approaches the line of scrimmage and continues throughout the route. The trickery can be taken to sophisticated levels.

However, this deception can be initially handled in an easy way. On all breaking routes (e.g., stop, curl, and comeback) that have a vertical stem (i.e., the path from the takeoff to the breakpoint), the receiver must sell deep. The receiver sells deep by looking downfield, accelerating off of the line as if he is heading for the end zone, using forward body lean, and always running full speed.

Consistently selling the deep route threatens a defender tremendously. He is threatened because a defender's greatest fear is to get beat deep for a touchdown. When a defender believes a receiver is able to run past him into touchdown territory, he will tend to drop back to protect against the deep threat, thereby enabling the receiver to run shorter routes against him effectively. Therefore, as routes are discussed, the theme of selling deep will be a constant.

Naming Routes and Packages

In this book, the most common names for routes are used. However, route names vary depending on the program. Additionally, some schools call by name packages of routes grouped together (e.g., smash as a stop route by the outside receiver and a corner route by the inside receiver).

Other programs indicate routes and packages by using numbers. When numbering is used, each route is assigned a number. Those numbers generally come from a passing tree. Some programs use even numbers for routes breaking to one side and odd numbers for routes breaking to the other side. Combining individual routes into packages can be done easily with numbers so that play calling is simplified (Figure 3-1).

Determining Depth of Breakpoints

Receivers can run their routes by either breaking at a certain number of yards or breaking at a certain number of steps. The preferred method is to have receivers run a designated number of yards instead of counting steps.

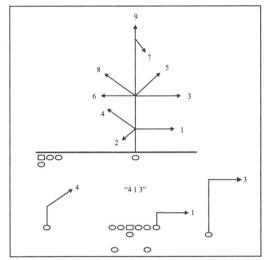
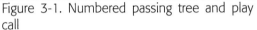

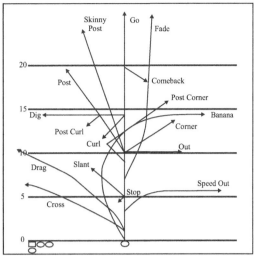

Figure 3-1. Numbered passing tree and play call

Figure 3-2. An example of a more detailed passing tree

Yards

Running a designated number of yards by using the yard lines on the field is easier than counting steps. Not having to count steps while running gives the receiver one less thing to think about. For example, on an out route, the receiver simply runs up the field to a depth of 10 yards, breaks, and runs his out path toward the sideline.

As the receiver approaches the line of scrimmage he visually spots the breakpoint by using the yard lines. However, he must be careful not to tip off the route by focusing on that spot. He must disguise looking at the breakpoint by making it a subtle part of his scan of the defense.

Because defenses are quickly adjusting to the modern passing game, it is important for receivers to be in the right location for the play called. Using yards instead of steps to determine route depth is optimal because receivers have different stride lengths. When a taller receiver runs eight steps, he will end up in a different spot than a shorter receiver who takes the same number of steps.

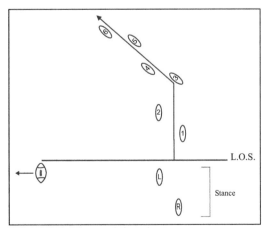

Figure 3-3. Steps of the slant route

One exception to this rule is the slant route. For timing purposes, teach the slant with steps because of the nature of the quick and short break, and because the pass is thrown immediately after the snap.

Steps

Gauging break depth by counting the number of steps is generally used in timing systems, as in the West Coast offense, where the quarterback's drop and the receiver's route are highly synchronized. For example, in this method, on a stop route the receiver plants with his outside foot on his third step and breaks back toward the quarterback, who has taken a three-step drop. While this works nicely for shorter routes, it gets more complicated to count steps when running longer routes. If you use this system, a trick for counting steps on longer routes is to have the receiver count the steps of only one foot instead of counting the steps of each foot. For example, a nine-step post becomes five steps by only counting each time the outside foot hits the ground.

Using this system, it also becomes very important for the receiver to start with either his inside or outside leg forward—depending on the route. To make the count come out right, the receiver may have to change his stance based on the route he is running, which could tip off the defender. Therefore, because of the difficulty in counting steps on longer routes and given the risk of tipping-off the defender, calculating depth using yards is preferred.

First Down—or Not

Whether you use steps or yards, it is important to teach receivers (and quarterbacks) to think about the yardage needed for a first down in crucial game situations. To guarantee the first down, the receiver needs to catch the ball past the down marker and not rely on gaining yards after the catch. In other words, if your stop route is normally five yards but you need six yards for a first down, your players should lengthen the route accordingly. A good rule of thumb in this situation is chains plus two yards.

Basic Routes

This section reviews 14 of the most common routes. The descriptions provide designated depths for the breakpoints of each of the routes. However, depths of routes are subjective and vary based on circumstances such as the age and ability of the players, and the offensive system. The splits that receivers should take are always normal splits, unless otherwise noted.

Slant

The receiver cheats his splits out toward the sideline and aligns with his inside leg forward in his stance. He pushes vertical to sell a deep route. On his third step, he plants his outside foot and breaks inside and upfield at a 45-degree angle. The receiver should expect the ball immediately after his break.

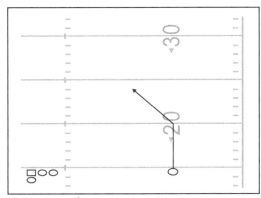

Figure 3-4. Slant route

Stop (Hitch)

This route is also known as the button hook. The receiver drives hard upfield to sell the deep route (fade or go). At a depth of five yards, he makes a hitch cut (Chapter 5) by planting with his outside foot and breaks at a 45-degree angle back toward the quarterback. Some programs make this break at six yards to allow more operating room for the receiver to come back to the ball, but the preferred method is to make the break at a depth of five yards for optimal timing with the quarterback. At the break, the receiver needs to square up (show his numbers) to the quarterback and immediately get his hands up to catch the football. If the ball is not there after the break, the receiver has two possibilities. One is for the receiver to keep coming back toward the quarterback at a 45-degree angle until he makes the catch. The alternative is for the receiver to throttle down and get open in the zone—usually by moving laterally to work away from the defender as he awaits the ball.

After the catch, the receiver makes a move—preferably outside—away from defenders, unless the ball placement or the defender dictates otherwise. It is important for the receiver to not lose ground after the catch, and to turn upfield on as tight a path as possible.

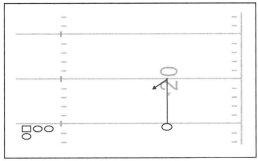

Figure 3-5. Stop route

Speed-Out (Quick Out)

The receiver cheats his splits to the inside to allow more room to catch the ball. He pushes vertical off the line of scrimmage to sell a deep route. At a depth of four yards, the receiver speed cuts off (rolls over) his outside foot (Chapter 5). As he rolls over his outside foot, he should get his head around quickly to look for the football. The receiver continues to bend the route up to a depth of six yards where the route flattens out. It is important not to drift upfield once the depth of six yards has been reached or that may open the play up to an interception.

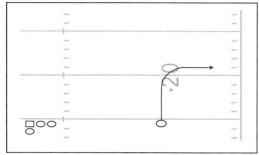

Figure 3-6. Speed-out route

Cross (Shallow)

The receiver cheats his splits to the inside to reduce the territory he has to cover to get across the field. He sells a deep route by releasing vertical off the line of scrimmage for two steps. He then speed cuts at an angle that will take him to a depth of six yards over the middle of the box (the area from tackle to tackle) and in front of the linebackers. The receiver then flattens the route, holds the route at a depth of six yards, and runs toward the far sideline.

Different offensive systems have different releases and aiming points at which the receiver reaches his designated depth. Instead of releasing vertical, some systems have the receiver take an immediate angle to the inside. Also, instead of the receiver reaching depth in the middle of the box, he may need to do so at either the nearside or the farside of the box. On all crossing routes, it is important not to drift upfield due to interception risk.

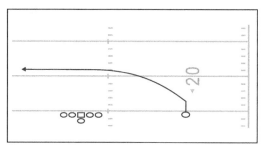

Figure 3-7. Cross route

Drag (Climb)

A drag route is typically run by a backside receiver when the quarterback is rolling out (or booting out) to the opposite side of the formation from the receiver's initial alignment. The receiver typically cheats his splits to the inside, takes off at an angle, and runs directly to the opposite hash mark at the appointed depth (e.g., 12 yards). The receiver then runs flat at this depth toward the sideline. It is important for him not to drift upfield, as that takes him farther away from the quarterback (who is already making a difficult throw on the run), and may open the play up to interceptions.

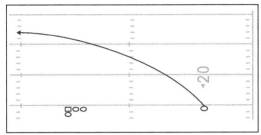

Figure 3-8. Drag route

Curl

The receiver pushes hard vertical to sell the deep route. At a depth of 12 yards, he makes his cut. The several variations to the top of the curl route are all based on trying to get the receiver to an open spot in the coverage. See Chapter 7 for a detailed description of the effectiveness of each variation versus different coverages.

Stick and Come Back at 45 Degrees

The most common curl cut is when the receiver sticks and comes back at a 45-degree angle. It is executed like a hitch cut. Therefore, an easy way to teach it—and the preferred method to initially teach this route—is as a stop route, only deeper. After the cut, the receiver keeps moving back down his 45-degree path toward the ball in flight. Coming continuously back toward the ball in flight and/or the quarterback helps the receiver gain separation from the defender. Following the maximum separation theory, the receiver should keep coming back until he catches the ball.

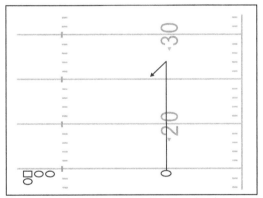
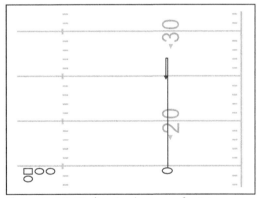

Figure 3-9. Curl: stick and come back at 45 degrees   Figure 3-10. Curl: retracing your footsteps

Retracing Your Footsteps

An alternative is to have the receiver plant and come straight back down the stem he has just run. This retracing-your-footsteps method means that the receiver is making a sharp 180-degree turn.

Curl Off of a Post Stem

Some programs threaten deep on a curl route off of a post stem. That is, the receiver runs straight up the field and breaks to the post at a depth of 10 yards. After going two or four steps on the post route, the receiver cuts to the curl by planting again off his outside leg and comes back on a direct line toward the quarterback. One significant advantage of running the curl off of a post stem is that it enables a receiver to convert this route to a post whenever defenders begin sitting on his curl route.

Throttle Down and Get Open

The final variation for the top of the curl route is for the receiver to throttle down and get open between defenders. Specifically, he breaks to the inside, opens up to the line of scrimmage, shuffles horizontally across the field, and remains in whatever void he can locate. The receiver may just sit at the point where he breaks if he is already open.

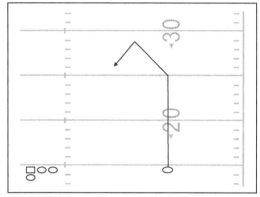 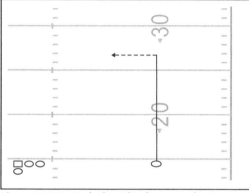

Figure 3-11. Curl: off of a post stem   Figure 3-12. Curl: throttle down and get open

Out (Square-Out)

The receiver cheats his splits inside to allow for more room to catch the ball. The receiver releases vertical off the line of scrimmage and sells deep. At a depth of 12 yards, he breaks at a 90-degree angle on a flat path directly toward the sideline. The break may be either:

- A plant with his inside foot and a turn of his upper body toward the sideline
- A quick chopping of the feet at the breakpoint and then the turn toward the sideline

The type of break used depends on the offensive system and the skill level of the receiver. Whichever type of break is used, the receiver should get his head and eyes around quickly and his hands up fast to make the catch. A speed cut may also be used at this depth if a sharp plant is not needed to shake a defender. Regardless of the type of cut, the receiver must be careful not to drift.

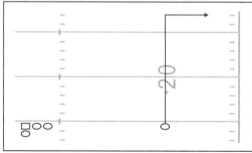

Figure 3-13. Out route

Square-In (Dig)

The square-in (dig) is the inverse of the square-out route described in the preceding section, and like the square-out may be run with either a basic plant or a quick chopping of the feet. Based on the offensive package and the defensive windows, different rules apply as to how far across the field to run and how fast to approach the middle of the field.

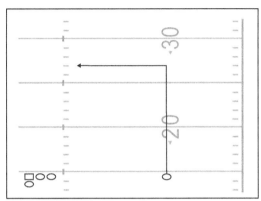

Figure 3-14. Dig route

Post

Regular Post

The receiver drives hard off the ball. At a depth of 10 yards, he plants with his outside foot, breaks inside at a 45-degree angle, and aims for the farside upright of the goalpost. In some systems, his aiming point is the middle of the uprights, known as "splitting the uprights."

Skinny Post

The technique for the skinny post is the same as the regular post. The only difference is that the aiming point for the receiver's route is the nearside goalpost.

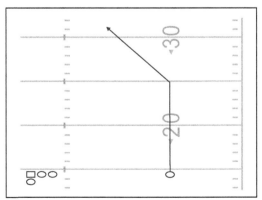 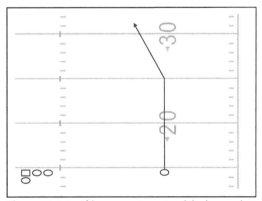

Figure 3-15. Regular post route (aiming point: farside upright)

Figure 3-16. Skinny post route (aiming point: nearside upright)

Corner (Flag)

This route is the inverse of the post. The receiver cheats his splits to the inside to allow for more room to catch the ball. The receiver bursts off the line of scrimmage, plants with his inside foot at a depth of 10 yards, and breaks at a 45-degree angle toward the sideline. Depending on the coverage, splashdown (where the ball is expected to be caught) is typically at a depth of 18 to 20 yards.

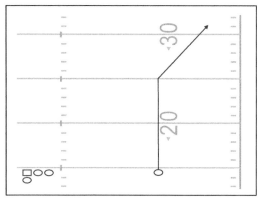

Figure 3-17. Corner route

Fade

The receiver pushes vertical off the line of scrimmage. At four to six yards, he bends his route to the fade stem. The stem of the fade is a vertical route run on the appointed landmark (normally the numbers). At a depth of approximately eight yards, the receiver starts looking for the ball so that he can begin to judge its flight path and adjust his route, if necessary. It is important that the receiver stays as long as possible on his vertical fade stem by heading straight upfield. However, he may have to move off of his landmark when he sees the ball's trajectory. He must remain at least five yards from the sideline (the five-yard highway) until the last possible moment, when he must adjust his route to make the catch (i.e., "let the ball fade you"). The quarterback is coached to throw this pass toward the sideline so that the only player who has a chance to catch it is the receiver. In most cases, he catches it over his inside shoulder at a depth of approximately 20 yards.

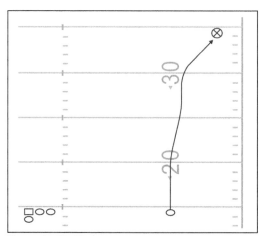

Figure 3-18. Fade route

Novice receivers tend to lose sight of the ball on this route, partly because their heads bounce too much as they run. Remind them to run on the balls of their feet to keep their heads steady and to improve your completion percentage in these instances.

Vertical (Go, Fly, Streak, Seam)

In this type of route, instead of selling deep, the objective is to actually go deep. The receiver expects the football at 20 yards or more. The terms—vertical, go, fly, streak, and seam—are virtually interchangeable except that a seam route typically refers to running vertical up the hashes. General landmarks for these routes are:

- Outside receivers run on the numbers.
- Inside receivers run on the hash marks (for high schools).

These landmarks are especially important for maintaining horizontal separation from defenders when several vertical routes are being run at the same time.

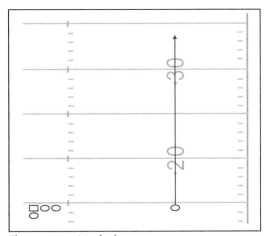

Figure 3-19. Vertical route

Comeback

This route is the inverse of the stick-and-come-back-at-45-degrees curl, but it is run deeper upfield. The receiver sprints up the field as though he is going for a fade or a go ball. At a depth of 20 yards, he plants with his inside foot and breaks back downfield

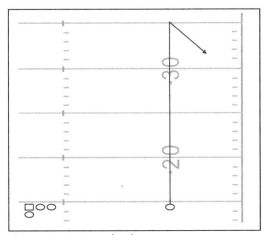

Figure 3-20. Comeback route

toward the sideline at a 45-degree angle. The ball should reach the receiver when he has taken just two or three steps after his break. To prevent an interception, he must keep coming back toward the football until the catch is made.

Alternatively, use a fade fake at a depth of approximately 16 yards immediately before the break. The receiver slightly bends his route as if starting to break on the fade ball. He makes the fake by quickly looking back for the football. He then executes his regular comeback break.

Banana Route

The banana route is a bent route; it does not involve a sharp stick or "plant." From the line of scrimmage, the receiver runs a semicircular route that starts toward the middle of the field and bends to a splashdown near the sideline at a depth of approximately 14 yards. The shape of the route resembles the shape of the fruit.

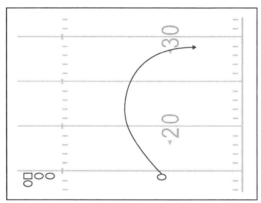

Figure 3-21. Banana route

Double-Move (Combination) Routes

Double-move routes are when aspects of two routes are combined into one. Coaches' imaginations can run wild in this area as long as their players are physically able to execute the plan. This section examines the more common double-move routes.

Stop-and-Go

The stop-and-go route is typically used after the defender has successfully begun to cover the stop route. In this route, the receiver runs to the normal depth of a stop route, plants, and turns, but does not take a step back toward the quarterback. Instead, he quickly flashes inside with his hands up and looks as if he is about to catch the football. The quarterback pump fakes in his direction. The receiver then quickly turns inside onto his vertical stem. The objective of the flash is to momentarily freeze the defender and gain enough separation between the receiver and defender so the receiver beats the defender deep.

A common variation is to have the receiver turn to run to the outside instead of the inside. He shows his numbers to the quarterback at the moment of the pump fake, pulls his outside shoulder and arm around, turns outside, and bursts upfield outside the defender. This method works best when the defender is playing with inside leverage and initiating contact off the line of scrimmage because the momentum of the turn and rolling off of the defender should enable the receiver to get separation from the defender. This maneuver is similar to the spin move, which will be discussed in Chapter 9.

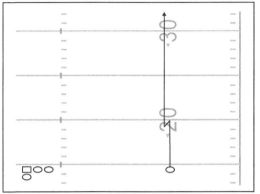

Figure 3-22. Stop-and-go route opening inside

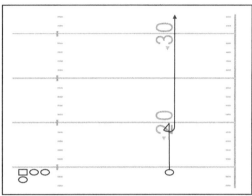

Figure 3-23. Stop-and-go route with an outside turn

Stalk-and-Go

The stalk-and-go is a combination generally used in the play-action passing game. While the quarterback and running back are faking the run, the receiver approaches the defender and engages in a stalk block. On this route, and only on this route, it is acceptable to have receivers lackadaisically release from the line to further sell the run. Next, as the quarterback prepares to pass, the receiver releases onto his go route. Needless to say, to get the timing fine-tuned takes more than a few practice reps.

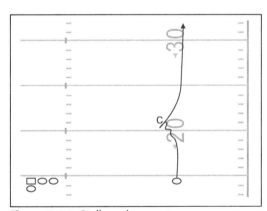

Figure 3-24. Stalk-and-go route

Post-Corner

In the post-corner route, the receiver sells the post route to the defender. Therefore, the post-corner route starts off with the same mechanics as the post route. Typically, the receiver makes the post break at a depth of eight yards. (Note that for timing reasons this break is slightly shorter than the usual post break.) He then runs two steps on the post stem. On the third step, he executes a corner-route break and aims at a 45-degree angle for the sideline.

From his work on the two separate and easier routes—the post and the corner—the receiver should be able to make each of the required moves independently. The trick is combining them in a very short space and time. Make sure that the receiver gets plenty of reps and uses all the correct mechanics on this route.

"PCP" (Post-Corner-Post)

The PCP route is a state-of-the-art extrapolation of the post-corner route. The technique of the route is identical to the post-corner until after the receiver runs two steps on the corner stem. On the third step of his 45-degree path toward the sideline, the receiver plants with his outside foot and breaks on a post path back toward the nearside goalpost.

It is difficult for a receiver to handle all the footwork as quickly as this route demands, but it can definitely be mastered with practice. A big benefit is that this route is virtually guaranteed to confuse and stupefy defenders as they become turned around (almost going in circles) and try to orient themselves to both the receiver and the ball. If you really want to mess with the defense, this is a good opportunity.

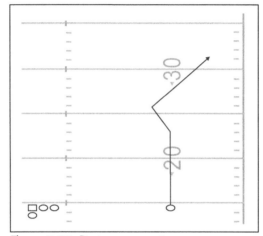

Figure 3-25. Post-corner route   Figure 3-26. Post-corner-post route

Dig Off of a Post Stem

In many systems, a dig route is another name for a square-in. However, this section refers to a double-move dig route (i.e., a dig route off of a post stem). The receiver runs a post breaking at a depth of 10 yards—his usual depth for a post route. He then continues on the post route for three steps. On the fourth step, he plants his outside foot, breaks inside, and comes flat across the field. Thus, the mechanics of the first cut are those of the post break. The mechanics of the second break are similar to those of the first break except that the angle of the aiming point has rotated. It is important to train receivers to come straight across the field once they have made their second break. Once again the mantra: drifting upfield can lead to interceptions.

Out-and-Up (Wheel, Chair)

This route is effective when the cornerback has started to sit on the speed out. The receiver runs a regular speed out, except that on the third step after his initial speed cut (in some systems the fifth step), he makes a second speed cut that enables him to run vertically up the field.

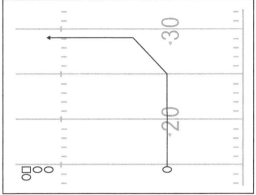

Figure 3-27. Dig route with a post cut

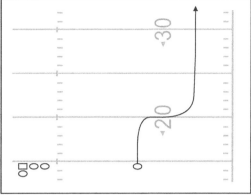

Figure 3-28. Out-and-up route

On his initial three-step path across the field, the receiver should look at the quarterback, who pump fakes to him. This fake helps freeze the defender and should allow the receiver to gain separation on the vertical part of his route. When running this route, the receiver must leave enough operating room for the quarterback's pass by making sure his route does not stray outside the five-yard highway.

Alternatively, this route may be run off of a square-out stem—especially in offenses that run more square-outs than speed-outs as their base routes. However, because of the footwork involved in the square-out break, it is a more time-consuming route and therefore the quarterback needs to have good protection.

Slant-Fade

This route is effective when the cornerback has started to sit on the slant route. The receiver executes a slant, but on the third step after his slant break, he plants with his inside foot and runs a fade stem, and then adjusts quickly to the ball in flight. This route is complicated to execute because the receiver must make a sharp and quick plant, and then accelerate immediately into high speed on the fade route. Otherwise, he will not be successful in eluding the defender. The slant-fade is more difficult than other double-move routes because the slant route does not provide any directional momentum toward the fade.

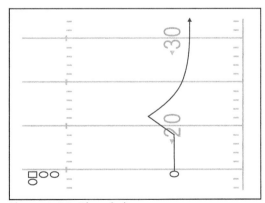

Figure 3-29. Slant-fade route

Screen Routes

Screen packages are generally used against aggressive defenses that get good penetration as well as against blitzing teams. A key rule for receivers on all screens is that the receiver must be behind the line of scrimmage when he catches the football. With linemen blocking downfield on this play, the forward exchange of the ball must be behind the line of scrimmage like a running play, or you will receive an illegal man downfield penalty.

Screens often involve a crack block (Chapter 8) by the second receiver on the same side of the formation as the screen-pass receiver. The three most common types of wide receiver screens are the middle screen, the bubble screen, and the quick screen.

Middle Screen

The middle screen may be executed by either the inside or outside receiver. After an optional jab step forward, the receiver releases flat down—but behind—the line of scrimmage toward the middle of the box.

The receiver must learn to judge the timing of the play's development. He synchronizes his arrival for the catch with the defensive linemen's rush to the quarterback and with the progression of the offensive linemen's downfield blocking. He catches the ball at a distance of two to four yards from the box, or in the box depending on the offensive system. Then he runs north-south through the middle of the field where the crease is being created by the blockers.

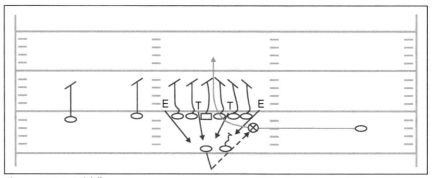

Figure 3-30. Middle screen

Bubble Screen

The bubble screen is typically run by the inside receiver, who opens with a couple of steps away from the line of scrimmage and moves out toward the sideline on a small and shallow semicircular path. This bubbling out is necessary for timing purposes and to give the quarterback a good angle to get the ball into the hands of the receiver before he reaches the line of scrimmage. An interesting variation is to simply have an off-the-ball receiver backpedal toward the sideline so that the quarterback has an easy pass to make. The bubble screen is generally used in conjunction with a crack block that is executed by the outside receiver on the linebacker or safety aligned over the inside receiver.

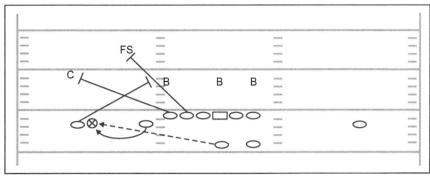

Figure 3-31. Bubble screen

Quick Screen

The quick screen is typically run by the outside receiver. The two versions of the quick screen are as follows:

- The first is so quick that the receiver does not even move from his original spot. He just opens up toward the quarterback and catches the ball.

- The other is similar to the bubble screen, but in the opposite direction. However, the area in which to maneuver is much more compressed than that of the bubble screen or middle screen. The receiver is running a route to the inside, but he must turn upfield in the nearside alley (hash marks) area, and not in the middle of the field. Because of the limited area, it is very useful to have the receiver widen his splits for this route. At the snap, the receiver opens inside and runs a narrow loop away from the line of scrimmage for a few steps. As he starts to turn upfield, the ball should be in his hands.

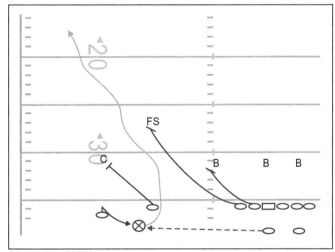

Figure 3-32. Quick screen

After the catch, the receiver accelerates past the line of scrimmage and up the alley where the running lane is being created. To get more yards after the catch, tell the receivers to work from the alley to the numbers and then to the sideline as they progress up the field. Doing so helps them to avoid the middle of the field, where all the defenders usually are.

Goal-Line Routes

The receiver needs to be especially physical when attempting to catch the football on the goal line. He should use his body as a shield between the defender and the ball as it comes toward him. Also, the receiver must keep moving if he does not immediately get the ball—because the defense is generally in a man-to-man coverage and the defender will be mirroring the receiver. If the receiver stands still, he can easily be guarded by his defender, which takes him out of the play.

Certain adjustments to routes must be made for success against the pressure of man-to-man defense and the smaller area of field available in goal-line situations. Four of the routes previously examined are also commonly used with these amendments in goal-line situations.

Slant

To run a successful goal-line slant, the receiver generally sells the fade route. He does so by getting an inside release with a double move by taking a single step to the inside, two choppy steps to the outside, and then continuing on to the slant (Chapter 4). Alternatively, the receiver can take an outside release in combination with the push-him-by-technique (Chapter 6). The receiver ultimately beating the defender inside and precise timing of the route and throw are essential for the success of this route.

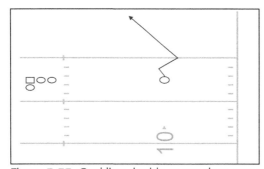 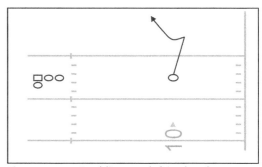

Figure 3-33. Goal-line double-move slant route   Figure 3-34. Goal-line push-him-by slant route

Fade

The aiming point for the goal-line fade is the pylon in the back corner of the end zone. Because the receiver has a shorter distance to cover on this fade, he can spend time misleading the defender early in the route. The receiver takes two choppy steps toward the defender's inside shoulder, as though releasing on the slant. Then, he plants off his inside foot and pushes into the fade route. During the route, the receiver keeps as much space as possible between himself and the sideline by running upfield with body lean into the defender (Chapter 6). He adjusts to the ball in flight as it nears splashdown at the back pylon.

Comeback

The receiver gets an outside release without giving up too much ground toward the sideline, sells the fade route, and plants with his inside foot. He then cuts and comes downfield at a 45-degree angle toward the sideline to gain separation from the defender. Ideally, the depth of the break is five yards beyond the goal line. This depth should allow enough room for the receiver to come back for the ball while still in the end zone. The quarterback's aiming point for the throw is the pylon in the front corner of the end zone.

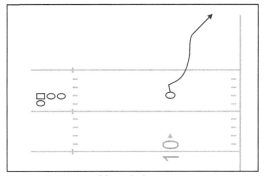
Figure 3-35. Goal-line fade route

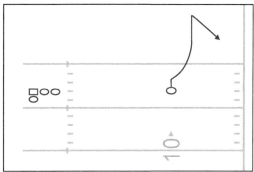
Figure 3-36. Goal-line comeback route

Speed-Out

Since in goal line situations the defender is usually in man-to-man coverage with inside leverage, the sideline is open for a speed-out. The receiver must narrow his splits somewhat but not so much that it is obvious he is making an out break. Again, precise timing between the quarterback and receiver is essential for the success of this route.

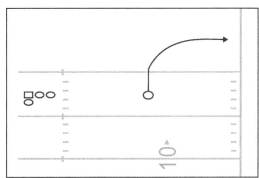
Figure 3-37. Goal-line speed-out route

Pick (Rub) Package

A pick (rub) is a combination route package with the outside and inside receivers. It occurs when one receiver "inadvertently" gets in the way of another receiver's defender to prevent him from making a play on that receiver. Pick routes are illegal at all levels of football. (Admittedly, most programs have at least one in their arsenal.) They can work like a charm when used sparingly and subtly. The key is to make sure the receiver who is doing the picking makes it look accidental by looking for the football. This play thus looks like natural chaos and no flag is thrown.

Traditionally, pick routes have been used when the defense is in a man coverage scheme. However, a good pick play must have an option that allows receivers to adjust to zone coverages when man coverage does not appear as expected. This adjustment also works when the defenders make a switch call (e.g., banjo) and adjust to crossing receivers by trading who they are covering man-to-man.

In a classic pick play used against man coverage with a zone adjustment, the inside receiver's responsibility is to pick the cornerback over the outside receiver to free him up for the catch. The inside receiver runs toward the cornerback and aims for the inside shoulder of that cornerback. The inside receiver must turn to look for the ball just before coming into contact with the cornerback. Looking back for the ball is the key to making the contact appear to be incidental and to avoid a penalty.

Simultaneously, the outside receiver runs to a depth of five yards, makes a hitch cut, and turns his head to find the inside receiver, who is running toward the cornerback. After the hitch cut, the outside receiver continues to a slant path by running underneath the inside receiver toward the alley. He should expect the ball as soon as he clears underneath the inside receiver. If the defender over the inside receiver stays with that receiver and the cornerback is successfully picked, the play will develop as planned.

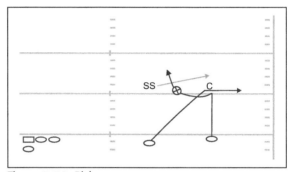

Figure 3-38. Pick route versus man-to-man coverage

This play can develop in two other ways:

- If the defenders stay in man coverage but adjust to the play by switching responsibilities (banjo), then no pick can occur. The inside receiver's adjustment is to continue on past his target defender and turn upfield and run to a fade path. This route thus becomes a wheel route, and the inside receiver must sell the speed-out route to beat the cornerback deep. The outside receiver runs his same route.

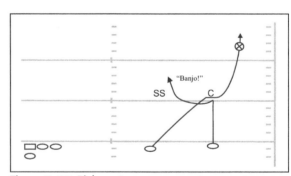

Figure 3-39. Pick route versus man-to-man coverage with a banjo call

- If the defenders bail on or before the snap, a pick becomes unnecessary. The inside receiver converts his route to a speed-out and expects the ball in the flat, since that is now the open area. The outside receiver converts his route and runs a slant route on top of the speed-out.

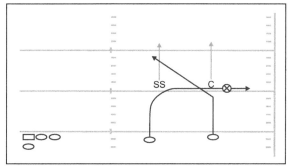

Figure 3-40. Pick route versus man-to-man coverage with cornerback bail

Drills

ABCs

Objective: To work on catching the football in a condensed area (mini-field) with very rapid repetitions. Several basic routes should be used each time this drill is run.

Equipment Needed: Four footballs

Setup: The coach stands on a yard line. The receivers form one line on each side of the coach and eight yards away.

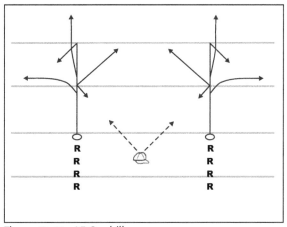

Figure 3-41. ABCs drill

Execution: The coach simulates the snap. The receiver to the right of the coach releases, runs the route, makes the catch, and accelerates upfield five yards. The same sequence is repeated to the left and again to the right. Receivers run each of the following routes:

- Stop route (which also works as the top of a curl)
- Slant route (which also works as the top of a post)
- Speed-out route
- The top 10 yards of a comeback
- Fade

Technique: The receiver starts from a proper stance, bursts off the line, runs the route making the correct break, and catches the football using proper hand technique. After the catch, the receiver makes a tight turn and quickly accelerates upfield.

Common Errors:

- Receivers do not run precise routes because they focus more on the catch than on correct route mechanics.
- Receivers do not execute their breaks correctly.
- Receivers do not catch the ball because they do not get their head and eyes around quickly enough.
- Receivers do not turn quickly and tightly upfield.
- Receivers do not properly adjust to the fade ball.

Things to Yell:

- "Sell deep!"
- "Run a crisp route!"
- "Stay low in the break!"
- "Head and eyes around!"
- "Tight turn!"
- "Adjust to the ball!"

Routes on Air

Objective: To improve a receiver's route-running ability, to fine-tune timing between quarterbacks and receivers, and to teach the plays to all the offensive skill players at one time

Equipment Needed: Eight footballs

Setup: Line up the skill players in a formation on the field. Use four quarterbacks in the middle of the field to simultaneously throw passes to each position (receivers, running

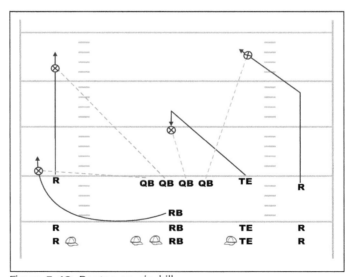

Figure 3-42. Routes on air drill

backs, and tight ends) as they run their routes. The coach needs to assign each quarterback a line of receivers to throw to, based on which play is being run. Every time you change plays, adjust the quarterback/receiver assignments as needed, so the quarterbacks are not crossing paths with their throws.

Execution: Use this opportunity to teach and then execute offensive pass plays. Players release at the snap and run their routes.

Technique: The receivers run the correct routes, execute the correct breaks, catch the football, and accelerate upfield.

Common Errors:

- Receivers run the wrong routes.
- Receivers do not make good cuts.
- Receivers do not make the catch.
- Receivers do not accelerate upfield.

Things to Yell:

- "Burst off the line!"
- "Sell deep!"
- "Run a crisp route!!"
- "Head and eyes around!"
- "Accelerate through the break!"
- "Let's make four catches!"

Variations:

- This drill can be executed on the goal line to give the receivers practice in red-zone scoring situations (slant, fade, comeback, and speed-out).
- Because several position coaches (running backs, tight ends, receivers, and quarterbacks) are involved in this drill, it makes sense for them to show various coverages while they coach. The coaches do not need to make plays on the ball after the snap, no matter how tempting that may be. They merely line up in selected defenses so that as the offense approaches the line they can practice quickly recognizing different coverages and learn to make adjustments and audibles. Coaches are still able to watch their players and make any needed corrections. However, by utilizing coaches in this way, you are working on routes and defense recognition at the same time.

One-on-One

Objective: To improve the receiver's ability to execute proper releases, run great routes while being tightly covered man-to-man, and catch the ball in traffic

Equipment Needed: Four footballs

Setup: Receivers align with a defender covering them. (Nothing takes a receiver's game up a notch faster than multiple reps with a defender right there with him.) The quarterback is in the middle of the field. You may use two lines of quarterbacks and receivers and throw to both sides at the same time. The defenders use a variety of different leverages and distances off the line during this drill.

Execution: The quarterback and receiver are told which route to execute. They run the play with the receiver focused on being physical, beating the defender off the line, getting open on the route, and securing the catch.

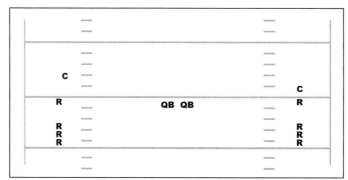

Figure 3-43. One-on-one drill

Technique: The receiver must start in a proper stance and with the correct splits, use quick physical release moves, run the correct route, catch the football, and accelerate upfield after the catch.

Common Errors:

- Receivers get jammed at the line and rerouted.
- Receivers do not execute proper breaks.
- Receivers do not gain enough separation from the defender during the route to be open for the catch.
- Receivers do not come back to the football when warranted.
- Receivers do not catch the ball.
- Receivers do not accelerate upfield after the catch.

Things to Yell:

- "Get off the jam!"
- "Don't let him mess with you!"
- "Run a good route!"
- "Keep moving!"
- "Concentrate! Radar lock on the ball!"
- "Adjust to the ball!"
- "It's yours and nobody else's!"

Variation: As well as in the open field, this drill can be executed deep inside the red zone from one to five yards out. Red-zone work gives receivers practice on routes such as the slant, fade, comeback, and speed-out in a goal-line situation.

RELEASES

Chapter Four

This chapter examines release techniques the receiver uses when he faces press coverage. Press coverage primarily occurs when a defender lines up in front of the receiver (anywhere from right in his face to four yards off of him) with the intent of making immediate contact to disrupt the receiver's route. A press defender usually appears when the coverage is either cover 2, man, or a hybrid (Chapter 7). In order to achieve the fastest and smoothest release possible by minimizing contact with the defender, the receiver must use a combination of techniques involving stance, hands, arms, and feet.

Which Way to Release?

The one general rule for selecting the direction (either inside or outside of the defender) the receiver should release to from the line of scrimmage is that for inside breaking routes, receivers release to the inside, and for outside breaking routes, receivers release to the outside. Like most rules, however, a few exceptions can be found (Chapter 7).

Whichever way the receiver chooses to release, it is important that you coach him to attack half the body of the defender as opposed to squaring up on the defender. If the receiver releases head-up on (directly at) the press defender, he will run straight into the defender. Attacking half the body gives the receiver a leverage advantage, which allows him to get around the defender more easily. Also, it is imperative that receivers not allow themselves to be manhandled and rerouted by the defender. The receivers must be physical and get upfield as soon as possible. "Get going, get upfield, and get hands off!"

Stance

The receiver should shorten his stance when he realizes a defender is going to press him. A shorter stance gives his feet less area to cover while making his initial moves. Shortening his stance thus enables the receiver to execute his jab steps and takeoff steps more quickly and to move off the line faster. The quicker footwork generated by this stance is a key component in breaking the jam.

Also, when the receiver shortens his stance by bringing the back foot closer to his front foot, he should bend his knees slightly more than usual. Shortening the stance thus gives the receiver a lower center of gravity and results in a more compact and powerful body position. Additionally, this position lowers the receiver's pad level and gives the defender less of a target to get his hands on during the jam.

Hands and Arms

Along with a shortened stance, the receiver should make sure that he has his hands and arms ready to attack the defender's hands and arms. In this ready position, the receiver should have his arms flexed, hands clenched, and hands higher than the defender's hands. When a defender presses the receiver at the line, a simple rule is for the receiver to have his hands six inches above the defender's hands, but not higher than the receiver's eyes.

Hands and arms are extremely important throughout each phase of the release move. The keys to successful hand and arm movements include strength, quickness, and aiming point. The most important of these components is quickness. If the receiver is not fast enough with these moves, he will end up locked in hand-to-hand combat with the defender at the line of scrimmage. The defender will have succeeded in his goal of disrupting the timing of the offense. You may be especially vulnerable if you are running a quick passing-game offense (e.g., the West Coast offense).

A key use of the arms also occurs at the end of each release move. As a part of his running motion, the receiver uses his elbow to help push off of the defender to propel himself upfield and gain additional separation. As the receiver runs by (i.e., gets on top of the defender), he keeps his elbows flexed and his arms aggressively pumping. The receiver naturally continues to attack the defender as he runs upfield. The elbows are thus a weapon not just for push-off, but also to continue the receiver's escape from the defender.

Figure 4-1. Elbow push-off

Dip-and-Rip

The dip-and-rip is an "oldie-but-a-goodie" release move. The following description is for a receiver who wants to release outside, but obviously the inverse can be done for an inside release:

- As the defender brings his hands up for the jam, the receiver punches aside the hands of the defender with his outside arm and a clenched fist. Suggested aiming points vary from right above the wrist to the middle of the forearm to the elbow of the defender. The preferred method is to target the middle of the forearm because it hurts the worst. If the receiver attacks aggressively like this early in the game, the defender will treat him with more respect.

- The receiver then dips his inside shoulder into the outside of the defender's body. The aiming point of the receiver's shoulder is the armpit of the defender.

- Next, he rips up and through the defender's outside shoulder with his inside arm, which is flexed at a 90-degree angle. This motion is similar to a full-body uppercut in boxing.

Figure 4-2. Rip through

- As he executes this ripping and punching up motion, the receiver swaps hips with the defender by stepping with his inside leg immediately beside the defender and bringing his hips past those of the defender (that is, he steps "through the defender"). He uses aggressive arm pumping to continue his escape.

Figure 4-3. Swapping hips

This technique of swapping hips is extremely important. It allows the receiver to get back onto the stem of his route and forces the defender into a trail technique. If the receiver does not get his hips past the defender's hips, he allows the defender to be in a position to slow his route.

Swim Move

Another "oldie" (but not so "goodie") release is the swim move. It used to be quite common, but it has fallen out of favor. It tends to leave the receiver's ribs exposed for the defender to attack. It is included here for completeness' sake, and because it is sometimes a good change-up—especially when a tall receiver is matched up against a short defender. The receiver is releasing outside:

- This initial hand attack is the same as the dip-and-rip. The receiver's outside hand and arm punch across to force the hands of the defender down and out of the way as he moves to jam.

- The difference is the inside arm of the receiver, which comes up almost vertically and then pushes through past the head of the defender in the motion of a swimmer's crawl stroke.

- As the receiver's outstretched arm comes over the defender and makes contact with his back, the receiver pushes the defender back toward the line of scrimmage and uses the same motion to help propel himself upfield.

- He swaps hips and uses aggressive arm pumping motion to continue his escape.

Figure 4-4. Swim move

Grab-and-Punch

The grab-and-punch incorporates some of the same concepts as the swim move, but it keeps the receiver in a more protected position. The receiver is releasing outside:

- The initial hand move is not a pushing movement. Instead, the receiver uses his outside hand to grab the outside forearm of the defender and pulls it down and across the defender's body toward his opposite hipbone.

- With the clenched fist of his inside hand, the receiver punches through. His punching arm moves almost parallel to the ground and skims directly over the outside shoulder or upper-arm area of the defender (depending on the height differential).

- As the receiver makes this vigorous punching motion, he swaps hips with the defender and uses his inside elbow to push himself upfield and away from the defender.

Figure 4-5. Grab-and-punch release

Because the movement of the punch is a low, horizontal, punch-through motion and not a high, over-the-head, swimming motion, the ribs and underarm areas of the receiver are better protected. Some coaches argue that it is virtually impossible to "grab" the defender's arm, due to the quick nature of this release. Therefore, some coaches teach an open-handed swat instead of a grab (swat-and-punch), but the overall technique is otherwise the same.

Other Hand Moves

Following are some less common hand moves that may be an addition to your arsenal for occasional use. These change-ups are useful because the receiver needs to keep the defender on his toes by being unpredictable.

Bat

What distinguishes this hand-release move is that the receiver uses both of his hands in a parallel motion. As the defender makes his jamming move, the receiver swats at the defender's forearms with his fists and arms in a vigorous, parallel, and downward-angled motion. Since the receiver is batting the defender's arms out of the way, a key to this move is that the receiver must have his hands higher than the defender's hands at the snap. The receiver then steps through with his inside leg, swaps hips, and continues the route.

Classic Swat

This technique is generally out of favor because of the increased physicality of defenders and receivers during press coverage. Because the classic swat involves open hands as opposed to clenched fists, it is not nearly as powerful. In this move, the receiver pushes the defender's hands away by slapping down with his palms. To be effective, quickness is the key. The swat must be used in conjunction with fast footwork.

Samurai

Samurai is a methodology for football that relies heavily on martial-arts techniques. It is fascinating material, but the amount of time needed to incorporate it into your program is extensive. Nonetheless, if you want to go state-of-the-art, or if your receivers are martial artists, an excellent resource is Mark Miller's *Developing Martial Arts/Grappling Skills in Defensive Linemen* (Coaches Choice). No receiver's tape is currently available, but these hand movements work for receivers, too.

Feet

The receiver needs to combine one of the hand moves with effective footwork to get off the jam. It is imperative that the receiver gets vertical as soon as possible while not giving up any ground as he makes his release against press coverage. He must have quick feet no matter what type of footwork he uses.

Speed Release

A speed release is a super-fast release that involves quick hands but no initial directional fake with the feet off the line. The receiver's feet simply start the running motion as his hands quickly strike the defender. The receiver should use the most effective angle to get by the defender and onto his route as quickly as possible. This technique is sometimes called an angle release. The angle of the path the receiver takes to release will differ based on the route he is running and the leverage of the defender. Sometimes this angle will be only slightly off the stem of the route, and other times it may be a drastic angle. A speed release tends to work well for receivers who have extremely fast takeoff speed and power. However, for others it can mean a protracted battle at the line of scrimmage. So be sure to install a variety of other release footwork options.

Single Move

This move is Deception 101. The receiver takes a slight jab step forward in the direction opposite of the release. This step is not a step downfield as if he were starting to run, but rather a small half-step accompanied by a slight head-and-shoulder nod in the same direction. The receiver then takes a regular burst step off the line of scrimmage with his other foot and incorporates one of the hand moves previously described. Of course, to be successful, the receiver must bring his hips parallel to or ahead of those of the defender (swap hips) to complete his release.

Double Move

The double move is the graduate degree of releases. It is not the easiest to learn, and it must be executed extremely quickly to be successful. When done properly, it is a stellar way to beat the defender. In this example, the receiver releases outside. First, he makes a small jab step to the outside, quickly followed by a jab step to the inside. The two jab steps must take place on the line of scrimmage and not upfield. Doing so guarantees enough cushion between the receiver and defender for the defender to see the double move and be deceived by it. It is important that the receiver gives a head-and-shoulder fake in each direction using as much hip motion as possible to help deceive the defender. The receiver incorporates his choice of hand moves. The last step is a burst step upfield and to the outside to begin the route.

The double move is especially effective after you have used the single-release move several times on the same defender. The double move is also very effective on the goal line against man-to-man coverage in conjunction with popular goal-line routes such as slants or fades.

Four-in-the-Hole

This rapid foot-fire movement is used to freeze defenders at the line of scrimmage. The name comes from agility drills that are done on a speed ladder. In this drill, the player takes four quick pounding steps in one square (measuring approximately 20 by 14 inches) of the ladder while vigorously pumping his arms in running motion before moving on to the next square.

Mimicking ladder work in this release, the receiver fires his feet up and down directly under his framework four times with quick and small motions. Use the four-in-the-hole release with rookie receivers while introducing hand moves. It is footwork they can easily do on the first day of practice so you can focus on the various hand techniques. In game situations, it tends to freeze the defender and get him back on his heels as he assumes the receiver is going deep. He also does not know which direction the receiver is going to release to. The limitation is that this release does not turn the defender's hips, and therefore the receiver could be a sitting duck for the defender's attack. Nonetheless, four-in-the-hole has been used very successfully by many programs, notably Southlake Carroll High School, the 2005 5A state champions in Texas.

Putting It All Together

While hand moves and footwork are discussed separately here for reasons of clarity, they are obviously combined in any release move off of the line of scrimmage. Most footwork techniques can be used in combination with most hand techniques. For example:

- Speed release and dip-and-rip
- Single move and dip-and-rip
- Single move and the swim move
- Single move and grab-and-punch

- Double move and dip-and-rip

- Four-in-the-hole and the swim move

- Four-in-the-hole and dip-and-rip

- Four-in-the-hole and grab-and-punch

Initially, you should pick one or two release moves and work those hard and consistently in both directions in order for receivers to get as fast as possible with them. However, as receivers gain experience, they can experiment with a variety of hand and foot combinations, and you and the receivers can even create new variations not listed in this section.

Back on the Stem

After the receiver executes his hand and foot moves, he must be sure to swap hips with the defender. For routes with a straight stem (like a post, curl, stop, fade, or comeback), the receiver must then get back on the stem of the route. In other words, he must not let the defender push him off his desired path. Getting back on top of the defender is especially important for young receivers who may be able to execute most of the release moves at the line but fail to get back on the stem. The consequence is that the derailed receiver is not in the correct location, which leads to incomplete passes and interceptions.

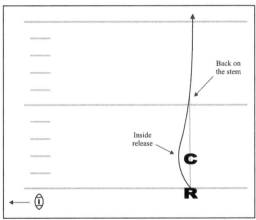

Figure 4-6. Swap hips and get back on the stem

Have a Plan

It is very important for receivers to come to the line of scrimmage with an aggressive plan for a successful release. As he runs to the line, the receiver needs to consider the following:

- Whether any stance adjustment is needed because of the release he is going to execute

- The direction he needs to release based on the route he is running and the leverage of the defender, as well as other things that may be occurring in the defensive or offensive package (e.g., the receiver must be careful not to release into his teammate's route)

- The optimal combination of hand moves and footwork technique that will enable him to obtain the quickest release and run the best route possible

Drills

Basic Release Drill

Objective: To teach the primary release moves to all receivers at one time

Equipment Needed: None

Setup: Have the receivers partner up, form two lines one yard apart, and face each other head-up. The distance between each pair should be three yards. One line is defenders, and the other is receivers. The coach stands 10 yards behind the defender line so that the receiver line can see him, but the defender line cannot.

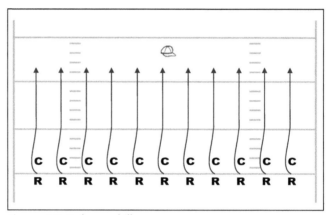

Figure 4-7. Release drill

Execution: Each hand and footwork release is designated by the coach.

- Speed release and dip-and-rip
- Single move and grab-and-punch
- Double move and dip-and-rip
- Four-in-the-hole and swim move

The defender puts his hands up to provide an aiming point for the receiver, but does not attempt to cover the receiver. The receiver executes the various release moves on the coach's signal and jogs upfield. The receivers and defenders then switch lines.

Technique: Receivers must execute each release with the proper technique, swap hips, and get back on the stem of their routes.

Common Errors:

- Receivers have trouble getting their hand and footwork synchronized.
- Receivers do not use enough force in their hand moves.
- Receivers do not get back on top of the defender or back on the stem.

Things to Yell:

- "Quick hands!"
- "Quick feet!"
- "Punch hard!"
- "Rip him!"
- "Get back on top of him!"

Advanced Release Drill

Objective: To practice live releases with all of the receivers at one time

Equipment Needed: None

Setup: The setup is the same as for the basic release drill. Have the receivers partner up, form two lines one yard apart, and face each other head-up with three yards between each pair. One line is defenders, and the other is receivers. The coach stands 10 yards behind the defender line so that the receiver line can see him, but the defender line cannot.

Execution:

- The coach signals which direction the receivers are to release to (left or right) and which footwork release to execute (one finger is single move, two fingers is double move, four fingers is four-in-the-hole, and fist is speed release). The hand move is the receiver's choice.
- On the whistle, the receivers execute the release on the defenders who are aggressively trying to jam them. The receivers get back on the stem of their routes and run upfield beyond the coach, who is standing 10 yards away.
- After the receiver group has completed each release once, the receivers and defenders swap places.

Technique: Receivers must execute each release with the proper technique, swap hips, get back on the stem of their routes, and sprint 10 yards upfield past the coach.

Common Errors:

- Receivers execute an ineffective move off the line.
- Receivers get caught up wrestling with the defender at the line and wasting time instead of having a quick and complete release.
- Receivers allow the defenders to disrupt them enough so that they get pushed off their route and run into the receiver next to them.

Things to Yell:

- "Quick hands!"
- "Smash his hands!"
- "Don't let him mess with you!"

- "Be aggressive!"
- "Swap hips!"
- "Get back on top of him!"

Variations: The coach has the defenders line up with different leverages and at varying depths.

Cone Release Drill

Objective: To improve the receiver's ability to make quick and complete releases in a short space to fully beat the defender

Equipment Needed: Six cones

Setup: Cones are lined up in a funnel shape on the field with the base eight yards apart and the top three yards apart. The distance from the base to the top is eight yards. A receiver lines up midway between the two wide cones with a defender lined up in press coverage on him. Defenders should vary their alignments over the course of the drill: inside, head-up, outside.

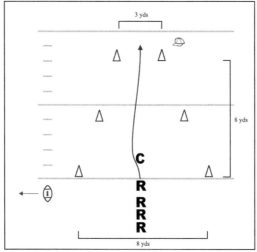

Figure 4-8. Cone release drill

Execution: The coach signals which direction each receiver is to break to. The receiver breaks the jam of the defender using footwork and hand moves. He pushes upfield quickly, gets back on the stem, and runs between the two cones.

Technique: Receivers need to have a release plan (and be able to articulate it to the coach, if asked) and release successfully (including getting hips swapped with the defender).

Common Errors:

- Receivers tend to wrestle with the defender at the line instead of having a finesse plan that gives them a quick and complete release.
- Receivers allow the defender to disrupt them so much that they cannot get back on the stem of their route (between the two top cones).

- Receivers may partially escape the defender, but not completely swap hips, enabling the defender to get back in the game and derail the route.

Things to Yell:

- "Attack!"
- "Quicker hands!"
- "Use a fake!"
- "Swap hips!"
- "Get back on top of him!"

Variations:

- Throw a ball to the receiver as he clears the second set of cones.
- Instead of the coach signaling the direction of the release, more experienced receivers should design their own release plan completely.

Speed Ladder: In-and-Out Drill

Objective: To improve the receiver's foot quickness off the line of scrimmage

Equipment Needed: Speed ladder

Setup: Receivers form a single line at the edge of the stretched-out speed ladder.

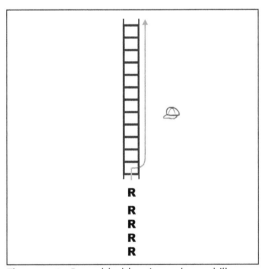

Figure 4-9. Speed ladder: in-and-out drill

Execution:

- The receiver begins in proper receiver stance with his left leg forward at the bottom of the ladder.
- He quickly foot-fires with both feet in the first square by placing one foot and then the other in quick succession in that square.
- The receiver then executes a drive step to the right side of the ladder and sprints parallel to the ladder to simulate the stem of a route.

- Next, the receiver executes the drill with the right foot up in the stance and drives off in the other direction.

Technique:

- Receivers begin in a proper stance.
- Receivers vigorously pump their arms (simulating running motion) in the first square of the ladder, as well as while running on the stem of the route.
- Receivers keep their eyes and heads up to see the defender.

Common Errors:

- Receivers foot-fire too slowly and not emphatically enough.
- Receivers look down at their feet.
- Receivers forget to pump their arms.
- Receivers do not use an aggressive drive step.

Things to Yell:

- "In and out!"
- "Arms!"
- "Quick feet!"
- "Push off!"
- "Accelerate!"

Variations:

- One variation is to have the receivers execute a four-in-the-hole move in the first square of the ladder. The receiver takes four quick foot-fire steps instead of just two in the first square of the ladder, and then continues on to the stem.
- Other drills that improve the speed and agility of receivers using the speed ladder can be found in the drills section of Chapter 5.

Broom Drill

Objective: To work on perfecting the shoulder dip in the dip-and-rip release

Equipment Needed: One broom per pair of receivers

Setup: Receivers partner up and line up facing each other. The receiver holds the broom horizontally behind his back and close to his body by locking the broomstick in place with his elbows and his back. His partner is lined up as a defender in press coverage ready to jam the receiver.

Execution: On the snap, the receiver executes a dip-and-rip release without being able to use his hands (his arms are occupied by holding up the broom behind his back). Make sure all receivers get practice releasing to each side.

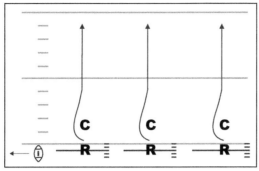

Figure 4-10. Broom drill

Technique:

- The receiver must get his shoulder dipped enough in the release so that the broomstick does not hit the receiver who is acting as the defender. The afflicted receiver will correct his partner's poor technique—so you don't have to.

- The receiver focuses on getting low into the dip and getting his body fully into the upward ripping motion.

- The receiver gets back on his stem as if running a route.

Common Errors:

- Receivers do not get enough of a dip, and hit the defender with the broomstick.

- Receivers do not use the force of their body to propel the ripping motion.

- Receivers do not get back on the stem of the route.

Things to Yell:

- "Dip!"
- "Get the shoulder down!"
- "Rip through!"
- "Get back on the stem!"
- "Knock it off!" (when the fist fight ensues)

CUTS AND SEPARATING

Chapter Five

This chapter analyzes the techniques of making cuts—or changes in direction—as the receiver runs his route. Cuts, or breaks, enable the receiver to gain separation from the defender, and are additionally important in route running so that the receiver is in the right place for the pass. The specific cuts described in this chapter are the hitch cut, post cut, square cut, speed cut, and double cut. In these cuts, proper technique enables the receiver to execute the fastest cut possible and gain maximum separation from the defender. It also prevents the receiver from slowing down, slipping, or falling down during the break. Correct technique is also important to help mislead the defender for as long as possible. Key aspects of good technique include correct footwork, body position, and use of the arms and the elbows.

Footwork in an Angled Break

To make an angled cut, the receiver needs to make a correct plant. If the receiver is making a cut to the right, he uses his left foot as the plant foot, and if he is making a cut to the left, he uses his right foot as the plant foot. In angled cuts, the receiver breaks by putting his plant foot to the ground, bending his knees, sinking his hips, and pushing off in the direction of the break. As the receiver breaks, he aims his toes of his plant foot in the direction of the cut and stays on the balls of his feet. The knee of the non-plant leg comes through and leads the weight transfer of the body in the new direction with a quick and powerful drive step.

In all angled cuts, it is very important for the receiver to keep his feet under his framework to ensure tightness in the break, and to prevent slipping and falling. Reaching with the plant foot outside the framework of the receiver's body to break makes him more prone to slipping because he is less stable. As with rising in the break, an over elongated or overbroad cut position slows the speed and reduces the precision of the break.

Body Position

Correct body position increases maneuverability and speed. The receiver needs to stay low and maintain correct running position to sell deep before the break. He must also maintain forward body lean throughout the break.

In all breaks, it is important that the receiver stays low and does not rise up as he cuts. Rising in the break signals to the defender that a cut is coming and eliminates any pretense that the receiver is going deep. Rising up also slows the speed of the break and makes the cut less crisp, thus reducing separation from the defender. In fact, to make sure receivers do not rise at the break, the preferred method is to coach receivers to sink at the break.

Use of Arms and the Elbow

Correct use of the arms before and during a break is essential, but it tends to be an undercoached and/or underlearned receiver technique. The elbow is a key component in providing the momentum for getting the body turned in the direction of the cut.

Arms Pumping

Active arms are important:

- To help the receiver disguise that a break is coming

- To initiate the break

- To prepare to catch the ball

Figure 5-1. Arm position during breaks

The receiver needs to have active arms during the break, which means his arms are continuously pumping in a natural running motion close to his body. Stress to your players the importance of keeping the arms moving right before the break, as even some college receivers have a tendency to let their arms fall down at their sides (i.e., dead arms). Dead arms tip off the defender that something is about to happen. Do not allow dead arms.

Figure 5-2. Error: dead arms during the break

Alternatively, receivers who are just learning to make angled breaks may instinctively bring their arms up to help them balance as they cut (i.e., airplane arms). This error often occurs with receivers who are playing too high. Keeping his arms tight into his body—especially when pulling the elbow to initiate the cut—helps the receiver make a more precise turn and accelerate through the break. Do not allow airplane arms.

Figure 5-3. Error: airplane arms at the break

To help receivers learn to keep their arms moving before, during, and after the break, the preferred method is to have them exaggerate this motion in practice by double pumping the arms at the break in drills so that in a game situation they naturally continue with at least some fluid movement.

Elbow

The natural arm-pumping motion thus continues throughout the break. At the breakpoint, the receiver pulls the elbow around (to the side he is cutting) to initiate the cut. The elbow action is a vigorous and overexaggerated arm-pumping movement (down and around) to change the receiver's momentum to the new direction. The momentum of the elbow coming through brings the receiver's shoulders around. The concurrent drive step in the new direction brings the hips around and gets the weight transferred in the new direction.

Head and Eyes

It is important for the receiver to keep his head up and not look down at his feet or the breakpoint. As a break is occurring, the receiver must get his head turned quickly and his eyes focused on the quarterback or the football in flight. Because a player cannot catch what he cannot see, it is imperative that the receiver learns to get his head around fast and his eyes searching for the football immediately.

Accelerate Through the Break

Receivers tend to concentrate so much on making the break correctly that they slow down. If the receiver slows down, the defender will realize the break is coming and will slow down as well. In addition, accelerating through the break provides the main window of opportunity to gain separation from the defender.

To help the receiver accelerate through the break, have him focus on the drive step by the non-plant leg. This strong and fast drive step is the key to initiating acceleration through the break, and should be as aggressive and powerful as possible. Of course, the receiver also needs to keep his arms moving and to stay low with his chest over his toes in a balanced, flexed, and powerful position—which enables him to change directions, and ensures that he gets his weight transferred quickly and smoothly.

After the Break: Hands Up to Catch

If a receiver maintains a natural running motion before, during, and after the break, his hands will be up and ready to catch any ball thrown at him—especially on quick-hitting routes like the hitch and slant. If his arms are down at his sides, he has greater distance to cover to get his hands in the appropriate catching position, and thus uses more time.

Mechanics of Specific Cuts

While there are many similarities in the mechanics of cuts, this section examines in detail the subtle variations between the specific types of cuts used in routes. Because of the importance of proper technique in making cuts, it is necessary to repeatedly drill the footwork and other mechanics in your most frequently used routes.

Hitch Cut

The hitch cut is used on routes such as the stop (hitch), curl, and comeback. It is one of the first breaks to introduce to receivers because the stop route is one of the shortest and most common routes.

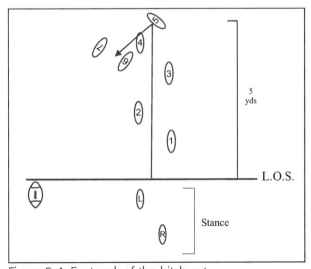

Figure 5-4. Footwork of the hitch cut

To use the stop route as an example, in the hitch cut, the receiver makes an angled cut, uses proper technique, and places his outside foot as the plant foot. The direction of the cut is at a 45-degree angle back toward the quarterback. After the receiver has made the plant with his outside leg and has turned around, he should be squared up to the quarterback, which is accomplished by bringing the plant leg around so that his feet are parallel and by showing his numbers to the quarterback.

Figure 5-5. Body and foot position at the start of a hitch cut

Post Cut

The post cut is used on post routes, corner routes, post-corner routes, and some dig routes. An advantage of this cut is that the receiver makes the plant and continues his running motion in a 45-degree angle upfield instead of slowing down to make a sharp turn back toward the quarterback. In the break, he plants and pushes off with his outside foot while giving a head-and-shoulder fake to the outside. As the inside leg comes through in his running motion, the toes of both of the receiver's feet should point toward his target. The break should be a fluid motion with minimal deceleration.

Figure 5-6. Body and foot position during a post-cut break

Figure 5-7. First step onto the post

Square Cut

Square cuts are sharp breaks made at a 90-degree angle. They are used on out routes as well as their inverse, in routes. Two sets of mechanics may be used. One is the square cut with a crisp plant, and the other is a square cut with choppy steps at the breakpoint.

Preferred Method

The preferred method to make a square-out cut is as follows:

- At the plant point, the receiver sticks the foot of the inside leg hard to the ground, bends his knees, and sinks his hips. As he sinks, the receiver keeps his arms pumping. He maintains forward body lean, and thus continues to sell deep until this plant has occurred.

- The receiver slightly angles his plant foot in the direction he is cutting, and then pushes off.

- He pulls his outside elbow around. The knee of the non-plant leg then leads the drive step in the new direction, which is at a 90-degree angle flat across the field. As he gets his head and eyes around, the shoulders and hips immediately follow to complete the weight transfer.

- Next, he brings the plant leg through so that his feet are parallel and runs flat down the line toward the sideline (perpendicular to his original path).

- Once the receiver has mastered the footwork mechanics, he needs to incorporate a head-and-shoulder fake in the opposite direction of the break as he initiates the plant with his inside foot.

The same technique is used for the square-in cut. The square cut is one of the most difficult breaks to teach novice receivers because of the tight footwork involved in a 90-degree break. They tend to round the break and drift upfield instead of a making a

Figure 5-8. Body and foot position of an out cut

sharp square cut. Rounding enables the defender to easily make an interception, leading to the common experience and expression, "the defender jumped the out route."

Alternative Method

If your receivers cannot master this cut effectively (and it will take many reps), you may want them to chop their feet before making the cut. This less precise movement offers more operating room for the turn. Sometimes this chopping motion actually freezes the defender and helps the receiver get open, similar to a stutter move after the catch (Chapter 9). The downside of this method is that the play takes more time to develop, and the defender may therefore have more of an opportunity to make a play on the ball.

Speed Cut

The speed cut is used on routes such as speed-outs and banana routes. It is one of the few cuts in football that does not involve an angular break.

Assuming the receiver is running a short speed-out and starts with his inside leg forward in the stance, he runs two steps forward. On the third step and continuing in his natural running motion, he rolls over his outside leg as he begins to climb to the proper depth of the route. As soon as the receiver rolls off his third step, he must get his head and shoulders around, look for the football, and continue flat down the line. No planting or deceleration occurs. He then typically has two yards to come to his final route depth (four bending to six), stop his climb, and hold his route flat.

An important coaching point in this cut is to teach the receiver to keep his breakside shoulder lower than the other shoulder. Doing so creates body lean in the direction of the break, and the resulting centrifugal force makes the break efficient, compact, and fast.

Double Cut

Double-cut routes contain the mechanics of two separate cuts within one route (e.g., the post-corner route). Some double-cut routes enable receivers to keep moving in the

Figure 5-9. Body and foot position during a speed cut

same general direction (e.g., the dig off a post stem). Some, notably the post-corner, require a 90-degree change of direction with only two steps in between. The complexity of double cuts results from:

- The very small operating area in which to maneuver
- The quick timing needed in order to execute two breaks within one route

To be successful in running double-cut routes, receivers need quick feet and overall agility.

A triple move is required on routes such as the PCP (post-corner-post) route, which contains the mechanics of three separate cuts within one route. The rapidity and the tightness with which the cuts must be made are challenging for receivers to execute. This set of moves is fun, but is very time-intensive to coach unless you are working with a truly select group of receivers.

Drills

Speed Ladder

Objective: To improve the receiver's foot coordination and quickness as well as to emphasize the use of the arms

Equipment Needed: Speed ladder

Setup: Receivers form a single line at the edge of the stretched-out single speed ladder.

Execution:

- The receivers run from the bottom of the ladder to the top as quickly as possible while placing one foot in each square. They then form a line at the top and come back in the opposite direction starting with the other foot.

- Next, the receivers foot-fire with two feet in each square from the bottom of the ladder to the top as quickly as possible. The first time through they lead with the left foot, and the second time they lead with the right foot.

Figure 5-10. Speed ladder drill

Technique:

- In the first phase of the drill, the receivers run with a natural fluid motion.
- In the second phase, the receivers use quick feet in each square and use an exaggerated arm pumping motion.
- Receivers need to push themselves to go as fast as possible while staying under control.

Common Errors:

- Receivers let their arms hang down instead of pumping.
- Receivers skip over squares or get tangled in the ladder because they are trying to go too fast.

Things to Yell:

- "Stay in control!"
- "Little steps!"
- "Arms!"
- "Quick, quick!"
- "Push yourself!"

Variation: A favorite variation is the "Icky Shuffle." The receiver places two feet in the first square (right, left), then the right foot outside the ladder, then two feet in the next square (left, right), then the left foot outside the ladder, and repeats through the entire ladder.

Sink-and-Pump Footwork

Objective: To train receivers to make correct breaks by keeping their feet under their framework, sinking their hips, and pumping their arms

Equipment Needed: Five cones and one football (optional)

Setup: Place the first cone five yards from the second one and each of the other cones four yards apart in a straight line. It is easiest to do this drill along the sideline or a yard line.

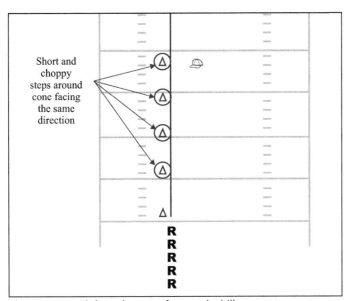

Short and choppy steps around cone facing the same direction

Figure 5-11. Sink-and-pump footwork drill

Execution: The receiver gets in his stance, bursts off the line, and runs to the right side of the first cone. He sinks his hips and moves to the front of the cone, then to the left side, behind, and back around to the right side while always facing the same direction. He takes tiny, choppy steps on the balls of his feet, and pumps his arms in an exaggerated way. When he gets back to the right side of the cone, the receiver pushes off hard, accelerates, and aggressively runs to each subsequent cone and repeats.

After a couple of reps, encourage the receiver to keep his head and eyes up and use peripheral vision to locate the cones. The first time the players run the drill, they usually need to look down to find and get a feel for the location of the cones.

Technique: This drill should be done at half-speed the first time and three-quarters speed the second. When the receivers have mastered the technique, have them progress to full speed and intensity.

Common Errors:

- The most common error is for receivers to do this drill with their feet too far apart and not take small enough steps around the cones.
- Receivers run the drill up too high and without shoulders over toes.
- Receivers master the footwork, but tend to forget to pump their arms.
- Receivers look down at the cones instead of keeping their heads and eyes up.

Figure 5-12. Sink-and-pump drill with correct form and eyes up

- Receivers try to go too quickly, do not use good technique, and do not stay under control.
- Receivers do a good job on the sides and in front of the cones, but they get rushed and sloppy on the backside.

Things to Yell:

- "Little feet, little feet!"
- "Quick feet!"
- "Sink your hips!"
- "Pump your arms!"
- "Little tiny steps!"
- "Keep your feet under your framework!"
- "Drive off the cone!"
- "Eyes up!"
- "Head up!"
- "Stay under control!"

Variations:

- This drill is great for getting in the face of unenergetic receivers and pumping them up. The coach faces the receiver, backpedals, and yells continuous encouragement and corrections to him as he executes the drill.
- The coach may throw a ball to the receiver as he rounds the last cone or intermittently during the drill.

Introduction to Square-Cuts

Objective: To introduce the receiver to 90-degree cuts. This drill teaches the receiver the initial plant footwork, and trains him to turn immediately in such a tight area that he is not later prone to drifting upfield.

Equipment Needed: None

Setup: Align the receivers facing the sideline and two yards apart with their right foot on a yard line. The coach stands facing the receivers on the same line.

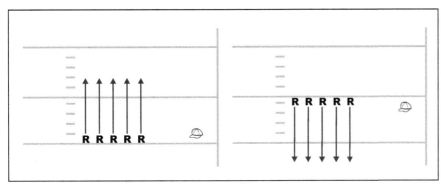

Figure 5-13. Introduction to square-cuts drill

Execution: On the first whistle, the receiver chops his feet in place and pumps his arms. On the second whistle, he plants with his right foot on the line, cuts to the left, and sprints five yards past the next yard line. Then, he lines up facing the same direction with his left foot on the line and comes back by planting with his left foot and turning to the right.

Technique: The receiver should vigorously chop his feet and pump his arms. He makes the cut with his plant foot on the line and slightly angled toward the new direction. Planting outside the line would mean planting outside the framework of the body. He gets his arm around, turns his head and shoulders in the new direction, drives through, shifts his weight, and runs full speed past the next yard line.

Common Errors:

- The receiver plants with his foot outside the line.
- The receiver rounds the break and runs into the receiver next to him.
- The receiver does not sprint full speed past the line.

Things to Yell:

- "Quick, quick!"
- "Foot on the line!"
- "Arms!"
- "Sharp cuts!"
- "Get out of the break!"

Carioca and Plant Drill

Objective: To work on the sinking of the hips needed to make correct breaks

Equipment Needed: None

Setup: Receivers line up three yards apart on a yard line. They face the sideline and the coach who is on the same yard line.

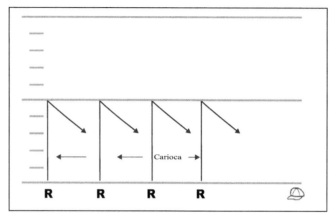

Figure 5-14. Carioca and plant drill

Execution: The receiver executes a proper carioca move while staying low. He moves laterally by stepping with the right foot crossing in front of the left. Next, he takes a lateral step with his left foot. Then, he steps with his right foot crossing behind the left foot. He continues this pattern for five yards up the field. At five yards, the receiver plants on the yard line (which helps him keep his feet under his framework), and makes a 45-degree cut back toward the coach.

Technique: The carioca move causes the receiver's hips to be open and working when he executes the break. The sinking motion needed in a proper break should flow naturally from the carioca motion. The receiver must plant with the proper foot (upfield foot), take a drive step with the non-plant leg, and accelerate out of the break.

Common Errors:

- Receivers rise up as they carioca instead of staying low.
- Receivers' arms go dead in the break.
- Receivers don't plant sharply and don't come straight back at a 45-degree angle toward the coach.
- Receivers reach too far to the side with their break foot, and don't plant on the line under their framework—and may even slip.

Things to Yell:

- "Stay square!" (during the carioca)
- "Eyes up!"
- "Sink the hips even more!"
- "Stay low!"

- "Hard sticks!"
- "Push off!"

Square Drill

Objective: To improve the receiver's ability to make 90-degree breaks, which are used in square-outs, square-ins, and so forth

Equipment Needed: Four cones and one football (optional)

Setup: Place four cones 10 yards apart in a square. The receivers line up at cone 1.

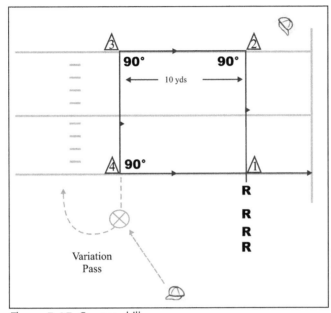

Figure 5-15. Square drill

Execution: Initially, this drill should be run at half-speed until receivers can master the correct footwork in the plants (which may take a while). Gradually work it up to full speed.

- The receiver starts in a correct stance at cone one and bursts off running to cone 2. He plants his outside foot (right foot) and makes a 90-degree break to the left.
- The receiver continues to cone 3, repeats the planting of his outside foot, and makes another 90-degree break to the left.
- The receiver does the same at cone 4.
- The receiver finishes the drill at cone 1.
- Riverside (flip) the drill.

Technique: At the breakpoint, the receiver needs to plant with his feet under his framework, and have his weight on the balls of his feet, his shoulders over his toes, and his arms continuously pumping. Pumping action should be exaggerated in this drill so that fluid and continuous arm movement carries over to game situations. He stays low and accelerates out of the break.

Young receivers will have lots of difficulty learning the footwork involved in this drill. At the time they are going to make the inside turn, have them imagine they suddenly see an ugly bug that needs to be smashed with their plant foot. They must stomp on the bug as part of their running motion while not losing speed or momentum into the turn. This visualization, while odd, helps them plant on the correct foot and get the correct quick weight transfer.

Common Errors:

- Receivers come up too high as they make their break.
- Receivers' arms tend to either hang down at their sides or fly up into the air.
- Receivers make their breaks with their feet too wide (splayed) apart, and they slip or even fall.
- Receivers look at the point where they are going to break.
- Receivers do not accelerate out of the break (in the full-speed version of this drill).

Things to Yell:

- "Sink your hips!"
- "Stay low!"
- "Keep your feet under your framework!"
- "No airplane arms!"
- "Pump your arms!"
- "Get your elbow around!"
- "Get your head around!"
- "Eyes up!"
- "Accelerate out of the break!"

Variations:

- One variation is to have a coach or extra player stand, bent at the waist, directly behind each cone to give eye contact to the receiver. When his eyes are met at this level, it confirms that the receiver is executing the break at the correct lower level. Also, the eye contact makes the receiver keep his head and eyes up and prevents him from focusing on the breakpoint.
- Another variation is to have the receivers plant only at cones 2 and 3, and then catch a ball as they pass cone 4. They should then turn tightly and accelerate upfield after the catch. This variation lets the coach check the following in a short period of time:
  - Stance
  - Two plants
  - Catching a head-on pass
  - Turning upfield and accelerating after the catch

- Because of the variety of activities occurring in this drill, the small space it is run in, and the fast pace of decelerations and accelerations required, you can get your receivers pretty pumped up. Especially if you give *continuous* feedback, this drill is another that is effective on days when you need to create some extra energy in your group.

- When your receivers have mastered this drill, put the bar up a notch. Have them execute this drill running inside instead of outside the cones. Doing so not only reduces their operating space, but also is a clear check of whether they are drifting upfield after they make their breaks.

M Drill

Objective: To improve the receiver's ability to make correct plants in stops, curls, and comebacks

Equipment Needed: Five cones and one football (optional)

Setup: Place four cones 10 yards apart to make a square, and place one cone in the middle of the square. The receivers line up at cone 1.

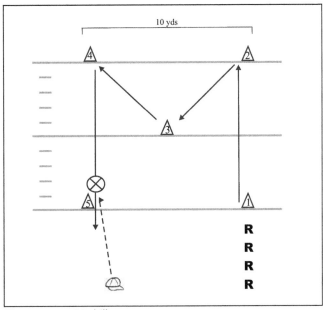

Figure 5-16. M drill

Execution: The receiver starts at the first cone and plants at cone 2, cone 3, and cone 4. As the receiver runs toward the fifth cone, the coach may throw him a football.

Technique: At each breakpoint, the receiver pushes off with his outside leg with that foot slightly angled in the direction of the break. He pulls his elbow around, gets his head and shoulders turned, and drives his non-plant knee in the new direction. He stays low in the break, keeps his feet under his framework, pumps his arms, and keeps his shoulders over his toes.

Common Errors:

- Receivers plant with the wrong foot.

- Receivers rise instead of sink in the break.
- Receivers slip (feet are not under their framework, or they are up too high).
- Receivers' arms go dead or they fly up at the break.
- Receivers look down at the break.

Things to Yell:

- "Stay in control!"
- "Keep your feet under your framework!"
- "Arms!"
- "Sink your hips!"
- "Stay low!"
- "Get your head around!"
- "Stay tight to the cone!"
- "Accelerate through the break!"

Variation: Intensify the pace by having the next receiver start as the receiver in front of him makes his second plant.

W Drill

Objective: To improve the receiver's ability to make 45-degree plants with the correct technique. These breaks are used in posts and corner routes.

Equipment Needed: Five cones and one football (optional)

Setup: This drill is run horizontally on the field. Place three cones 10 yards apart on a yard line. Place two cones on the next yard line in between the three cones so that the cones are staggered and delineating the five points of the W. The receivers line up on the yard line behind the first cone.

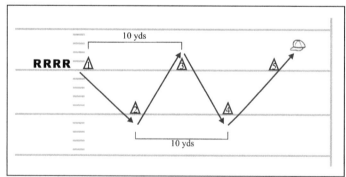

Figure 5-17. W drill

Execution: The receiver starts at the first cone and plants at each of the three middle cones.

Technique: At the breakpoint, the receiver pushes off his outside foot as he pulls his elbow around, turns his head and shoulders around, and drives his knee in the new direction. The receiver needs to sink in the break. He must stay tight to the cone, keep his feet under his framework, pump his arms, keep his shoulders over his toes, and accelerate in and out of the breaks.

Common Errors:

- Receivers do not plant with the correct foot.
- Receivers rise instead of sink in the break.
- Receivers slip (feet are not under their framework, or they are up too high).
- Receivers' arms go dead or fly up.
- Receivers look down.

Things to Yell:

- "Stay in control!"
- "Keep your feet under your framework!"
- "Smaller steps!" (at the break)
- "Arms!"
- "Sink your hips!"
- "Pull your elbow through!"
- "Eyes up!"
- "Get your head around!"
- "Accelerate through the break!"

Variation: Intensify the pace by having the next receiver start as the receiver in front of him makes his first or second plant. As each receiver runs toward the last cone, the coach may throw him a football.

Star Drill

Objective: To improve the receiver's ability to execute a variety of different plants (all in one drill)

Equipment Needed: Seven cones and one football (optional)

Setup: Align three cones seven yards apart in a straight line along a yard line. The middle cone is the star cone. Put one cone seven yards in front of and one cone seven yards behind the cone to the right of the star cone. These cones are identified as cones 1, 2, and 3. Put one cone seven yards in front of and one cone seven yards behind the cone to the left of the star cone. These cones are identified as cones 4, 5, and 6. The receivers line up 10 yards away and facing the star cone.

Execution:

- The receiver gets in a stance, releases to the star cone, executes a hitch/curl cut, runs through cone 1, and continues to the back of the line at the starting position. He then completes the same cut in the opposite direction to cone 4, and continues to the back of the line at the starting position.

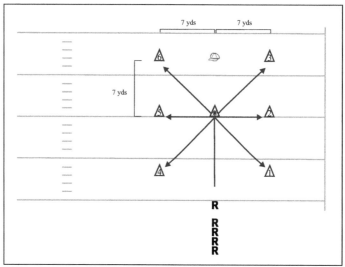

Figure 5-18. Star drill

- Next, the receiver gets in a stance, releases to the star cone, executes a square cut, runs through cone 2, and continues to the back of the line at the starting position. He then completes the same cut in the opposite direction to cone 5, and continues to the back of the line at the starting position.

- Now, the receiver gets in a stance, releases to the star cone, executes a post/corner cut, runs through cone 3, and continues to the back of the line at the starting position. He then completes the same cut in the opposite direction to cone 6, and continues to the back of the line at the starting position.

Technique: This drill works stance, takeoff, and major plant types (hitch/curl, square-in/square-out, and post/corner). Key technique points include keeping the feet under the framework, sinking the hips, pumping the arms in the break, pulling the elbow around, planting off the correct foot, and accelerating out of the break.

Common Errors:

- The receiver slows down at the breakpoint instead of accelerating through the break.
- The receiver's plant is too wide and/or overelongated.
- The receiver has dead arms or airplane arms.
- The receiver looks at his breakpoint instead of keeping his eyes up.
- The receiver does not get his head and eyes around quickly enough.

Things to Yell:

- "Keep your feet under your framework!"
- "Arms!"
- "Eyes up!"
- "Use your elbow!"
- "Get your head around!"
- "Accelerate out of the break!"

Variation: A football may be thrown to the receivers as they complete the footwork part of each segment of this drill.

Line Drill

Objective: To work on the receiver's technique on his curl and comeback cuts, as well as gaining yards after the catch (Chapter 9). This drill works well to ensure that receivers make sharp breaks and start running north-south immediately after catching the football. The use of the three-yard-line window shows concretely how tight of a turn a receiver is able to make.

Equipment Needed: Two footballs and three cones

Setup: This drill is run horizontally on the field. The first cone is on a yard line, and the receivers make a line behind this cone. The second cone is five yards to the side and two yards upfield from the first cone. The last cone is five yards down the field from the second cone on the adjacent yard line.

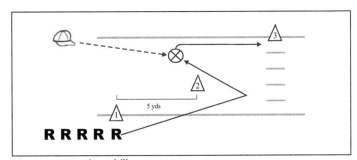

Figure 5-19. Line drill

Execution: From the start at cone 1, the receiver runs to cone 2 and executes a curl plant around the cone. The coach throws a football to the receiver as the receiver takes his second step back toward the coach. After he catches the ball, the receiver quickly turns and gets upfield, staying inside of the field stripe. He accelerates and bursts past cone 3.

Technique: The receiver must sink his hips, pump his arms, plant decisively, come back toward the coach, and then turn tightly and accelerate upfield.

Common Errors:

- The receiver freezes after the break and does not come back toward the ball to meet it.
- The receiver rises in the break.
- The receiver has dead arms or airplane arms.
- The receiver does not accelerate upfield after the catch.
- The receiver is not able to turn upfield tightly enough to avoid crossing the yard line.

Things to Yell:

- "Sink your hips!"

Figure 5-20. End of cut and ready to catch the ball

Figure 5-21. Turning upfield

Figure 5-22. Accelerating upfield

- "Get your head and elbow around!"
- "Accelerate out of the break!"
- "Come back to the ball!"
- "Tight turn!"
- "Accelerate after the catch!"
- "Finish!"

Variation: If you are working with inexperienced receivers, start with the second cone positioned one yard from the first yard line. As they improve, move the cone to the standard position. With high-level players, you can move the cone to three yards out, so their area to maneuver in after the catch is only two yards.

Chute Drill

Objective: To improve the receiver's ability to stay low during the breakpoint of a route (curl, out, and in)

Equipment Needed: One offensive-lineman, single-man chute and two footballs

Setup: Align the receivers on a yard line. Set the chute eight yards in front of them with the taller end of the chute facing the receivers. The coach acts as the quarterback.

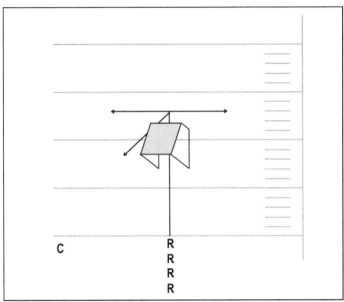

Figure 5-23. Chute drill

Execution: On the snap, the receiver runs the vertical stem of a curl route through the chute. As soon as he exits the chute, the receiver makes his curl cut and comes back to the ball. The receiver makes the catch and gets upfield. Next, he runs an in route and then an out route through the chute, using correct footwork in the break.

Technique: When passing through the chute, the receiver should keep his shoulders over his toes and must get low enough so he does not hit his head on the chute. He executes a correct cut at the breakpoint while accelerating through the break. He catches the ball, which is thrown immediately after the break.

Common Errors:

• Receivers do not get low enough, and therefore hit their heads on the chute.

• Receivers slow down while going through the chute.

• Receivers do not make a precise cut at the breakpoint.

• Receivers let their arms go dead during the break.

Things to Yell:

- "Get low!"
- "Accelerate through the break!"
- "Pump your arms!"

Variations:

- Align a defender in press coverage on the receiver as he releases. This variation simulates a game situation and gives the receiver even more to think about during the drill.
- Alternatively, align a defender holding a hand shield approximately two yards deep beyond the chute. The receiver runs through the chute and executes a stalk block on the defender. This variation works on the receiver's ability to stay low as he initiates a stalk block.

STEMMING AND OTHER MID-ROUTE TECHNIQUES

Chapter Six

At the line of scrimmage, a receiver either battles his way off the line, or, if no defender is in his face, has a free release. As he then runs the stem of his route, he must mislead, control, and evade the defender(s) covering him. This chapter examines a variety of mid-route techniques a receiver can use for stemming.

Square Up the Defender

A basic introductory rule of stemming a route is to square up the defender, which means that during the initial part of the route the receiver should run in the direction of the defender and straight toward the middle of his body. Coaches frequently use the phrase "attack his technique" to remind receivers to square up the defender.

The advantage of squaring up the defender is that the receiver's head-up position gives him the ability to break in any direction. For example, if the receiver is running a square-in route and the defender is playing with inside leverage, the defender is standing right where the receiver is headed. If the receiver runs his route without squaring up the defender, the defender will merely backpedal. Then, when the receiver makes his break, the defender will be in position to make an easy play on him and/or the ball. However, if the receiver squares up the defender, the defender will still backpedal, but the receiver's new head-up position enables him to get to the inside and be open on this route.

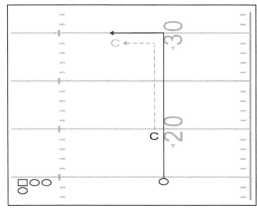 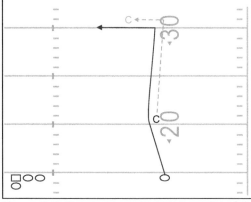

Figure 6-1. Error: receiver running a square-in without squaring up the defender

Figure 6-2. Receiver running a square-in while squaring up the defender

Additionally, squaring up the defender every time prevents tipping off to the defense which way the receiver is going to break and the direction of the route. That is, if the receiver runs straight at the defender on every route, he will keep the defender guessing each time. Also, when the receiver squares up on the defender, he reduces the ability of the defender to maneuver in between the receiver and the quarterback (i.e., slip underneath the receiver). Slipping underneath the receiver allows the defender to be able to jump the route and make an interception.

Squaring up the defender is thus the first and easiest stemming technique to teach receivers so that they have a basic framework. However, as discussed in Chapter 7, rules on stemming can be taken to higher levels of sophistication and intrigue. For instance, in some routes receivers should be taught to run at the defender's inside or outside shoulder instead of running straight at the middle of his body.

Body Lean With Contact

One technique a receiver can use to control his defender is body lean with contact. The receiver uses this technique to keep the defender away from the area he is ultimately going to run to. Body lean with contact means the receiver leans into the defender in the direction away from his ultimate break as the two run down the field together. In this duel, the receiver must fight to keep pushing into the defender with enough vigor to make sure the defender does not significantly disrupt the stem of the receiver's route by pushing back. This technique is usually used in conjunction with a push-off technique (discussed later in this chapter).

Body lean with contact is often used, but it is imperative to use it on the fade route. The receiver must continuously body lean into the defender, so he does not get pushed into the five-yard highway until he separates from the defender to catch the ball.

Weave Technique

In addition to physically pushing into the defender, body lean can be used with no contact at all. Specifically, this weave technique is used when the defender is either backpedaling in front of an oncoming receiver or in a trail technique (i.e., running on the hip of or closely behind the receiver). In weaving, the receiver leans his body (head and shoulders) and slightly bends the stem of the route in the direction opposite of his true break/route.

When the defender is backpedaling and the receiver bends the stem of the route in the opposite direction, it increases separation at the breakpoint because the defender has more territory to cover after reacting to the break. When the defender is in trail technique and the receiver bends the stem of the route in the opposite direction of his break, the defender's momentum in the off direction increases separation from

Figure 6-3. Weave: the receiver bends his stem to the opposite direction

Figure 6-4. Weave: at the breakpoint

the receiver at the breakpoint. In either scenario, the weave technique makes it difficult for the defender to recover in time to make a play.

Figure 6-5. Weave: separation from the defender

Push-Him-By

The push-him-by technique is another stemming technique. It may be used when the defender is running even with the receiver or tight on his hip, and the receiver needs to break in that direction. As the receiver makes his break, he pushes the defender by him and further upfield by putting his hand on the lower back of the defender and propelling him forward. The receiver then breaks underneath. The push must look like a part of the receiver's natural running motion or a penalty may be called.

This technique is typically used on angular breaking routes such as the out, in, stop, curl, slant, and post. It is often used as a Plan B when the receiver has not been able to release in the optimal direction at the line of scrimmage. For example, if the receiver cannot get an inside release while running a curl route, he can use the push-him-by technique at the breakpoint to get open.

The push-him-by technique can only be used if the defender is right on the receiver's hip or even with him. If the receiver has gained too much separation by beating the defender, the receiver would have to slow down at the break of the route to wait for the defender to catch up and then push him by. Therefore, the buzz phrase for the push-him-by technique is: "Don't beat him too badly!"

Push-Off

The push-off is another move a receiver makes to propel himself away from a defender who is even with him or on his hip at the breakpoint. The receiver pushes off the defender by using his elbow and/or forearm (e.g., the receiver uses his inside elbow to push-off an inside defender at the break of an out route). The push-off must be done with enough force to gain separation. The push-off must also be disguised by the receiver's normal running motion so that he does not receive a penalty for offensive pass interference. Remember the earlier discussion of the importance of pumping the arms in the break? Among its other purposes, this pumping motion helps disguise the push-off.

The push-off is commonly used in routes such as the out, in, post, and corner. While this technique works effectively on the out and the in, it works optimally on the post and the corner because in those routes the receiver can execute this pushing-off technique completely in stride as he runs.

One receiver who had this move down to an art form in the 1990s was Michael Irvin of the Dallas Cowboys. Watch some of his film and see the variety of techniques he used to make successful push-offs. His football philosophy was that he simply would not take no for an answer—and his aggressive push-offs underscore that point.

Head-and-Shoulder Fake

Head-and-shoulder fakes are used to gain separation from the defender without contact. This combined move should be a small and quick motion. Young receivers tend to overexaggerate head-and-shoulder fakes, which can slow down the speed of their route. A very quick nod and a slight dipping of the shoulders is all it should take to mislead a defender who is primed to respond to the smallest movement of the receiver.

Head-and-shoulder fakes are generally made in one direction as the receiver initiates his break in the opposite direction. However, a simple head bob can work almost magically for selling deep. Running on his vertical stem, the receiver nods his head slightly forward to indicate acceleration downfield and then breaks the route off underneath. Interestingly, since this fake is so subtle and natural, defenders may bite on it even more than they do on more dramatic fakes.

Mid-Route Dip-and-Rip

In Chapter 4, the dip-and-rip was examined as a key release move at the line of scrimmage. It can also be effective as a mid-route maneuver when defenders are playing off and/or sitting in zone coverage.

As the receiver approaches a defender on an outside breaking route, he dips his inside shoulder and rips up and through the defender's outside shoulder with his inside arm and elbow similar to the release at the line of scrimmage. However, this motion is fluid and is part of the running action, so it has no initial hand action like in the dip-and-rip release move. When you introduce this technique, an extremely common error is for a receiver to get entangled with the defender—almost like he is blocking—instead of quickly ripping through the defender and moving upfield.

Figure 6-6. Mid-route dip-and-rip

Drills

Mid-Route Dip-and-Rip

Objective: To improve the receiver's ability to use the mid-route dip-and-rip to stay on the stem of his route when a defender is sitting in his path

Equipment Needed: Ten cones and two footballs

Setup: Align a defender head-up over a receiver at a depth of eight yards. Place four pairs of cones one yard apart in two-yard increments on a vertical path through which the receiver runs the stem of his route. Place the last two cones at 10 yards from the line of scrimmage.

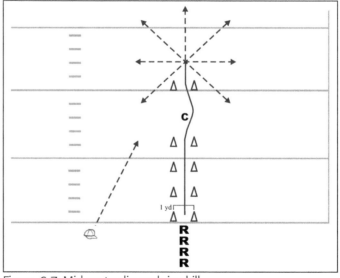

Figure 6-7. Mid-route dip-and-rip drill

Execution: The receiver aligns, releases, executes a mid-route dip-and-rip around the defender, gets back on the stem (between the last two cones), and finishes the route. The coach assigns the route and throws the ball. This drill is run with routes that break at a depth of 10 yards or more (e.g., curl, square-in, out, post, corner, comeback, and go).

Technique: The receiver takes a proper stance and bursts off the line. At the point of contact, the receiver dips his shoulder and rips through the defender using the proper inside or outside release for the route. Then he gets back onto the stem, makes the correct break, catches the football, and accelerates upfield.

Common Errors:

- The receiver does not burst off the line and run full speed toward the defender.
- The receiver does not use proper dip and rip technique, gets tangled up with the defender, and does not finish his route quickly enough.
- The receiver does not get back on the stem of the route (between the two last cones) before the breakpoint.

Things to Yell:

- "Accelerate off the line!"
- "Dip your shoulder!"
- "Get off him!"
- "Get back on the stem!"

Weave

Objective: To improve the receiver's weaving ability

Equipment Needed: Five cones and one football (optional)

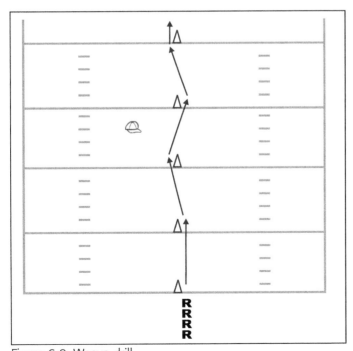

Figure 6-8. Weave drill

Setup: Place each cone five yards apart in a straight line.

Execution: The receiver aligns in a proper stance, bursts off the line, and runs a tight path around the cones. He accelerates through the finish.

Technique: The receiver uses proper weave technique by shifting his weight fluidly as he passes each cone. He rolls over the inside foot and pushes off his outside foot as he changes direction at each cone. He simultaneously dips his inside shoulder for maximum speed and tightness in the weave.

Common Errors:

- The receiver tries to plant his foot instead of rolling off of it, which breaks his stride and slows him down.
- The receiver loops around the cones instead of taking a tight path around them.

Things to Yell:

- "Stay close to the cone!"
- "Eyes up!"
- "Lean!"
- "Dip your shoulder!"
- "Accelerate!"
- "Finish strong!"

Variation: The coach may pass the receiver a football to catch as he rounds the last cone.

ROUTE ADJUSTMENTS VS. MAN AND ZONE COVERAGES

Chapter Seven

In order for the receiver to release correctly and run the most effective route possible, he must factor in the following:

- The type of route he is running
  - Whether it is an inside or outside breaking route
  - Depth of the route
  - Type of break in the route

- The defensive coverage
  - The leverage of his defender (head-up, inside, or outside)
  - The depth of his defender
  - The eyes of his defender
  - The alignments of the other defenders

Because of the myriad of factors to be considered, teaching a receiver how to successfully run his route versus different coverages cannot be done quickly. What follows is a guide to recognizing the main coverages, and what the defenders' duties are while playing that coverage. Then, a detailed review follows on the key ways to successfully run each basic route against:

- Man
  - Press man
  - Loose man

- Zone
  - Cover 2
  - Cover 3
  - Cover 4

In the sections where routes versus coverages are analyzed, the options are listed from easiest to most complex and/or the most used to the more obscure. This list is by no means exhaustive.

MAN

Man-to-man coverage is used:

- When the defense thinks their players match up favorably in one-on-one duels with the respective offensive players so that they can contain them.
- When the defense is blitzing and the number of defenders is insufficient to cover all the defensive zones.
- When the defense is less concerned about the pass and more concerned about defending the run. In this situation, the defensive scheme leaves the

cornerback to cover the receiver one-on-one so that the other defenders can focus on stopping the run.

- Often in goal-line and short-yardage situations to allow more defenders to focus on the run, and to minimize the cushion between the receiver and defender for short passes.

The three main types of man coverages are as follows:

- Pure man is when no deep safeties are employed. It is often used when one or more players are blitzing.
- Man free is when each player is manned up on an opponent—except for the free safety, who plays deep in the middle of the field.
- Man-under-two-deep is a combination of man and zone coverage with the cornerbacks and linebackers playing man and two deep safeties covering the deep halves of the field.

Cornerbacks may play:

- *Press man:* Aligned over the receiver typically at a depth of four yards or less, and initiating contact with the receiver to disrupt his route. In some cases, defenders may play with press-man alignment, but bail at the snap and use loose-man technique.
- *Loose man:* Aligned off the receiver typically deeper than four yards and covering the receiver man-to-man. In some cases, defenders may play with loose-man alignment, but step up after the snap and use press-man technique.

Some key indications that the defense is playing man-to-man are:

- Cornerbacks are aligned with inside or head-up leverage.
- Cornerbacks have their eyes fixed on the receiver, and are not looking at the quarterback at all.
- Cornerbacks' bodies may be slightly angled toward the receiver.
- Cornerbacks try to force the receiver outside to use the sideline as a second defender (i.e., neutralize the receiver by working him out of bounds).
- When a receiver motions during the cadence, one defender follows him wherever he goes as opposed to a couple of defenders bumping over to adjust responsibilities.
- No deep players are involved (pure man).

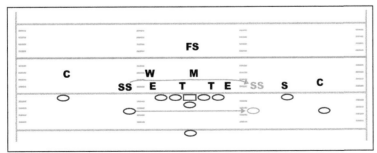

Figure 7-1. Defender in man-to-man following his man in motion

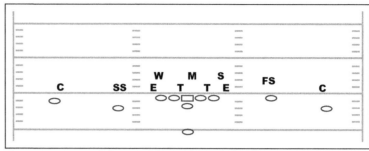

Figure 7-2. Man defense with no deep defenders

Some other indications that the defense *may* be playing man-to-man are:

- One defender is deep in the middle of the field (man free).
- If the defense blitzes, it may indicate man coverage.

Factor It All In

Receivers can't just fixate on one of the rules alone to determine whether it is man or zone coverage. Receivers need to factor in all available data to make sure they make the right call. Receivers must always:

- Check the number and location of the safeties.
- Check the leverage of the cornerback.
- Check the eyes of the cornerback.

For example, if one safety is in the middle of the field and the cornerback is head-up, these factors could imply either man or zone coverage. The determining factor is when the receiver looks at the cornerback's eyes. If the cornerback is focusing on the receiver, it is man coverage, and if the cornerback is looking inside toward the quarterback, it is zone.

Press Man

In press man, the cornerback is typically at a depth of four yards or less and usually crowding the line of scrimmage as much as possible so that he can immediately make contact with the receiver. This is also referred to as bump-and-run coverage. Usually, the cornerback lines up inside or head-up on the receiver and may be cocked to the sideline, so he can easily jam the receiver while already having his hips turned to run with the receiver. Since the cornerback's intent in press man is to disrupt the route that the receiver is running as well as to prevent the receiver from making a catch, the cornerback usually has his hands up ready to make contact with the receiver at the snap.

ROUTE ADJUSTMENTS VERSUS PRESS MAN

Stop Versus Press Man

Option #1—Press Man (Inside): The receiver takes what the defender gives, pushes vertical upfield, and uses a head fake to gain separation. At the breakpoint, he uses the push-him-by technique to get open.

Option #2—Press Man (Inside): The receiver attacks the defender's framework with one step in his direction. He then pushes vertical and uses the push-him-by technique at the breakpoint.

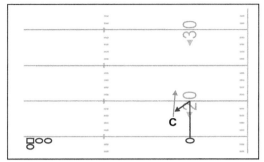
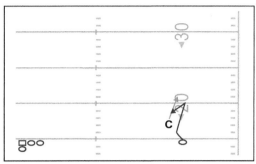

Figure 7-3. Stop route option #1: Press man inside leverage

Figure 7-4. Stop route option #2: Press man inside leverage

Option #3—Press Man (Inside): The receiver uses single-move footwork with a jab step to the outside at the line to turn the defender's hips. He then slips underneath the defender. He pushes vertical upfield while staying on the stem with body lean, makes the break, and comes back to the football.

Option #4—Press Man (Head-Up): The receiver gets an inside release using any hand move and a speed release. He then pushes vertical upfield, and stays on the stem by using body-lean technique, makes the break, and comes back to the football.

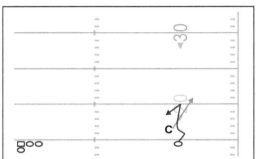
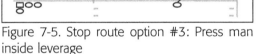
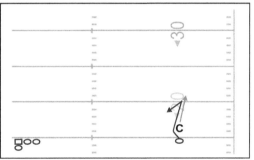

Figure 7-5. Stop route option #3: Press man inside leverage

Figure 7-6. Stop route option #4: Press man head-up leverage

Slant Versus Press Man

Option #1—Press Man (Inside): The receiver pushes vertical off the line and sells a deep route. At the breakpoint, he uses the push-him-by technique to throw the defender by, plants, and continues on the slant route path.

Option #2—Press Man (Inside): The receiver incorporates the double-move footwork concept in the slant route by taking one short jab step toward the defender, and then two quick steps upfield slightly to the outside to sell the fade or other deep route. He thus gets the defender to turn his hips. He uses the push-him-by move if needed, and then continues on the route.

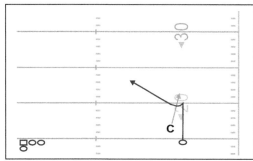 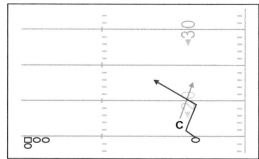

Figure 7-7. Slant route option #1: Press man inside leverage

Figure 7-8. Slant route option #2: Press man inside leverage

Option #3—Press Man (Head-Up): The receiver fights for an inside release with hand moves and a speed release. He uses body-lean technique to push vertical, and cuts to the slant at the breakpoint with an elbow push to create separation.

Option #4—Press Man (Head-Up): The receiver gets an inside release by using a single-move technique with a jab step to the outside at the line. Doing so turns the defender's hips, and the receiver slips underneath the defender. He then uses body lean to stay on the vertical stem and makes the break with an elbow push to create separation.

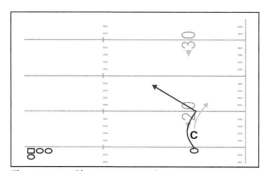

Figure 7-9. Slant route option #3: Press man head-up leverage

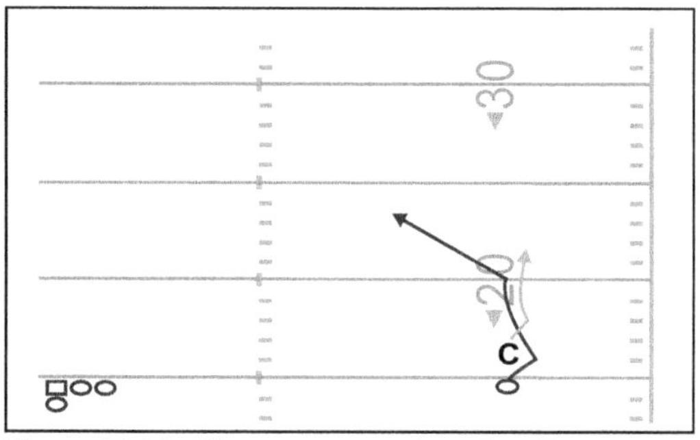

Figure 7-10. Slant route option #4: Press man head-up leverage

Option #5—Press Man (Head-Up): The receiver uses the double-move footwork by taking one short jab step inside and then two quick steps upfield to sell the fade or other deep route. Doing so gets the defender to turn his hips. Then the receiver continues on the route. It's got to be quick.

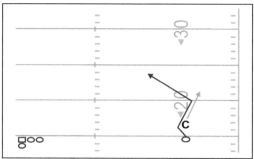

Figure 7-11. Slant route option #5: Press man head-up leverage

Curl Versus Press Man

Option #1—Press Man (Inside): The receiver fights for an inside release with single-move footwork and hand moves. He pushes vertical with body lean as he gets back on the stem of the route. At the breakpoint, he sticks and comes back to the football.

Option #2—Press Man (Inside): If the receiver cannot get an inside release, which is Plan A on an inside breaking route, he takes what the defender gives and pushes vertical upfield. He must be effective in selling the deep route. At the breakpoint, he uses the head bob and the push-him-by technique to get open and come back to the ball.

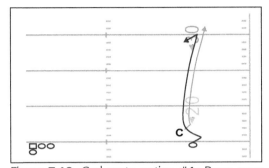
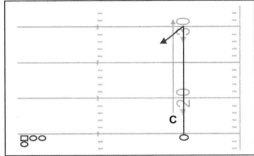

Figure 7-12. Curl route option #1: Press man inside leverage

Figure 7-13. Curl route option #2: Press man inside leverage

Option #3—Press Man (Head-Up): The receiver gets an inside release using any hand move and a speed release. He then pushes vertical upfield and stays on the stem by using body-lean technique, makes the break, and comes back to the football.

Option #4—Press Man (Head-Up): The receiver releases inside by using single-move footwork at the line to turn the defender's hips and get him outside. He then pushes vertical upfield while staying on the stem with body lean, makes the break, and comes back to the football.

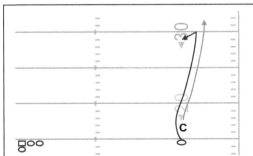
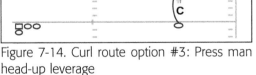
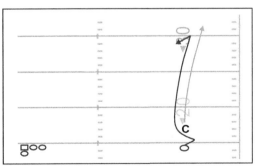

Figure 7-14. Curl route option #3: Press man head-up leverage

Figure 7-15. Curl route option #4: Press man head-up leverage

Square-In Versus Press Man

Option #1—Press Man (Inside): The receiver fights for an inside release with single-move footwork and hand moves. He then pushes vertical with body lean to get back on the stem of the route, and uses a head-and-shoulder fake to the outside at the breakpoint.

Option #2—Press Man (Inside): The receiver takes what the defender gives, and pushes vertical upfield. He must be effective in selling the deep route. At the breakpoint, he uses the push-him-by technique and breaks flat down the line across the field.

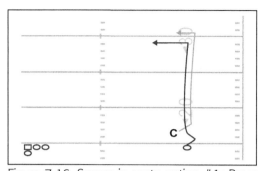 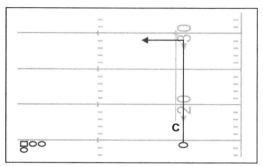

Figure 7-16. Square-in route option #1: Press man inside leverage

Figure 7-17. Square-in route option #2: Press man inside leverage

Option #3—Press Man (Head-up): The receiver gets an inside release using a hand move and a speed release. He then pushes vertical upfield, stays on the stem by using body lean technique, makes the break, and continues flat down the line across the field.

Option #4—Press Man (Head-Up): The receiver uses hand moves and single-move footwork at the line to turn the defender's hips. He then pushes vertical upfield while staying on the stem with body lean, makes the break, and continues flat down the line across the field.

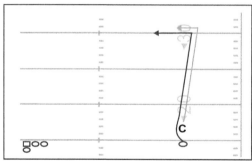 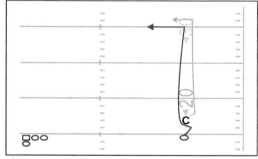

Figure 7-18. Square-in route option #3: Press man head-up leverage

Figure 7-19. Square-in route option #4: Press man head-up leverage

Post Versus Press Man

Option #1—Press Man (Inside): The receiver takes what the defender gives, and releases straight upfield. The receiver sells a corner route, and therefore the stem of the route actually has a slight bend toward the outside. He then uses weave technique and a head-and-shoulder fake to the outside at the breakpoint to get the defender on his outside hip. If the receiver has been effective in selling the corner route, the defender will break to the outside after the fake. The receiver then continues to the post.

Option #2—Press Man (Inside): The receiver fights for an inside release with single-move footwork and hand moves. He pushes vertical with body lean to get back on the stem of the route. At the breakpoint, he makes the break to the post.

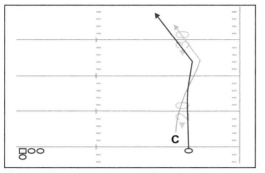

Figure 7-20. Post route option #1: Press man inside leverage

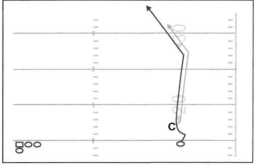

Figure 7-21. Post route option #2: Press man inside leverage

Option #3—Press Man (Head-Up): The receiver uses hand moves and an inside speed release. He pushes vertical with body lean to get back on the stem of the route. At the breakpoint, he makes a head-and-shoulder fake to the outside and breaks to the post.

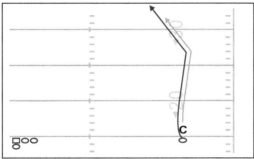

Figure 7-22. Post route option #3: Press man head-up leverage

Dig (Post Stem) Versus Press Man

Option #1—Press Man (Inside): The receiver takes what the defender gives, and releases straight up the field. He makes the post break and sells the deep post route with a head bob so that the defender will be running full speed to the post during the second break. He then uses the push-him-by technique at the second breakpoint and cuts straight across the field.

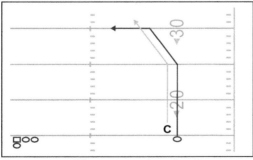

Figure 7-23. Dig route option #1: Press man inside leverage

Option #2—Press Man (Head-Up): The receiver fights for an inside release with a speed release and hand moves, pushes vertical with body lean on the defender, and works back onto the stem. At the first breakpoint, he makes a post break with a head fake to the outside. At the second breakpoint, he sells the deep post with a head bob, makes the cut to the dig route, and proceeds straight across the field.

Option #3—Press Man (Head-up): The receiver fights for an inside release with single-move footwork and hand moves, pushes vertical with body lean on the defender, and works back onto the stem. At the breakpoint, he makes a post break with a head fake to the outside. At the second breakpoint, he sells the deep post with a head bob, makes the cut to the dig route, and proceeds straight across the field.

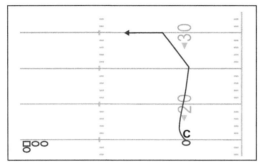 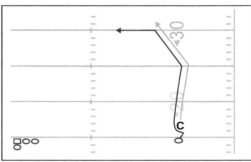

Figure 7-24. Dig route option #2: Press man head-up leverage

Figure 7-25. Dig route option #3: Press man head-up leverage

Out Versus Press Man

Option #1—Press Man (Inside): The receiver releases vertical upfield. He may use body-lean technique to keep the defender on the inside. At the breakpoint, he makes a cut with an inside head-and-shoulder fake. He may use a slight elbow push to create separation at the breakpoint. He then continues flat down the line toward the sideline.

Option #2—Press Man (Head-Up): The receiver gets an outside release using any hand move and a speed release, pushes vertical upfield, and gets back on the stem by using body-lean technique. He makes the break with an inside head-and-shoulder fake and continues flat down the line. The receiver may use an elbow push to create separation at the breakpoint.

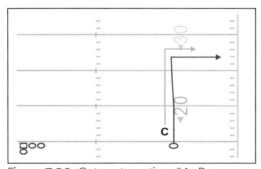 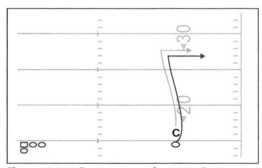

Figure 7-26. Out route option #1: Press man inside leverage

Figure 7-27. Out route option #2: Press man head-up leverage

Option #3—Press Man (Head-Up): The receiver uses a hand move and single-move footwork at the line to turn the defender's hips. He pushes vertical upfield, and may use body lean to get back on the stem. The receiver makes the break with an inside head-and-shoulder fake and continues flat down the line. He may use an elbow push to create separation at the breakpoint.

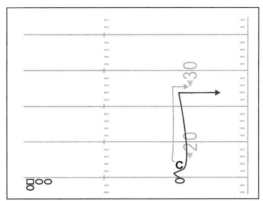

Figure 7-28. Out route option #3: Press man head-up leverage

Fade Versus Press Man

Option #1—Press Man (Inside): The receiver takes an outside release by simply releasing vertical and using a hand move if necessary. He may use body lean to keep working the defender to the inside. The receiver stays on the stem until he needs to adjust toward the sideline to the ball in flight.

Option #2—Press Man (Head-Up): The receiver gets an outside release using a speed release and any hand move. He then pushes vertical upfield, gets back on the stem by using body lean to the inside, and adjusts to the football.

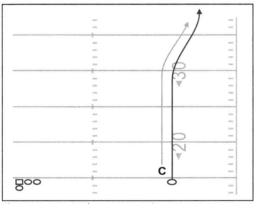 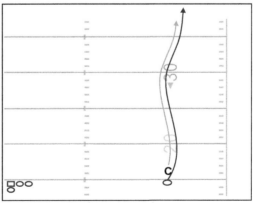

Figure 7-29. Fade route option #1: Press man inside leverage

Figure 7-30. Fade route option #2: Press man head-up leverage

Option #3—Press Man (Head-Up): The receiver uses single- or double-move footwork at the line to turn the defender's hips. After his release, he pushes vertical upfield while staying on the stem by using body lean and adjusts to the football.

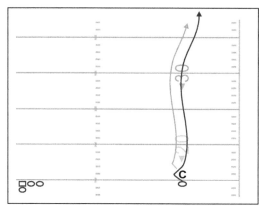

Figure 7-31. Fade route option #3: Press man head-up leverage

Comeback Versus Press Man

Option #1—Press Man (Inside): The receiver releases vertical upfield, and uses body lean to the inside if needed. Five yards before the breakpoint, he may slightly bend his route toward the fade and briefly turn his head as if to look back for the ball. At the breakpoint, he makes the comeback cut toward the sideline.

Option #2—Press Man (Head-Up): The receiver gets an outside release using a speed release and a hand move. He may use single-move footwork if it's really fast. He then pushes vertical upfield and gets back on the stem by using body lean to the inside. Five yards before the breakpoint, he may slightly bend his route toward the fade and briefly turn his head as if to look back for the ball. At the breakpoint, he makes the comeback cut toward the sideline.

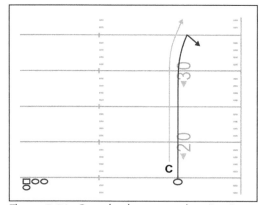 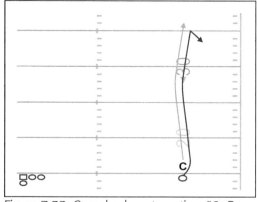

Figure 7-32. Comeback route option #1: Press man inside leverage

Figure 7-33. Comeback route option #2: Press man head-up leverage

Loose Man

If a defender is playing loose man (from a depth of more than four yards), it generally means that he respects the speed of the receiver. The same leverage rules apply to recognize loose man as press man. The defender's assignments are the same, except that he is not initiating contact with the receiver at the line of scrimmage.

ROUTE ADJUSTMENTS VERSUS LOOSE MAN

Stop Versus Loose Man

Option #1—Loose Man (Inside): The receiver runs the stem directly at the defender to push him deeper. He squares him up and uses a head bob to gain separation. He then makes a hitch cut and comes back to the football.

Option #2—Loose Man (Inside): The receiver pushes at the defender's outside shoulder for two yards and bends the route slightly outside to get the defender's hips turned. At the appointed depth, the receiver cuts and comes back to the football.

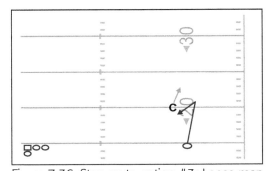

Figure 7-34. Stop route option #1: Loose man inside leverage

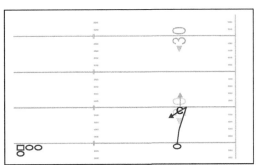

Figure 7-35. Stop route option #2: Loose man inside leverage

Option #3—Loose Man (Inside): The receiver angles his regular route slightly to the outside to simulate a fade stem. He does so to get the defender's hips turned. At the appointed depth, the receiver cuts and comes back to the football.

Option #4—Loose Man (Head-Up): If the defender is four to five yards off, the receiver sells deep and runs toward the defender's outside shoulder for the first two yards. He then bends the route outside to further turn the defender's hips. The receiver breaks at the appointed depth and comes back to the football.

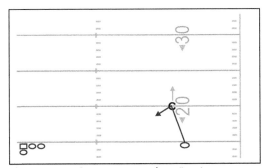

Figure 7-36. Stop route option #3: Loose man inside leverage

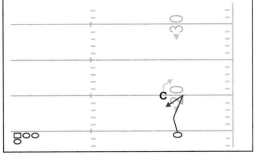

Figure 7-37. Stop route option #4: Loose man head-up leverage

Option #5—Loose Man (Head-Up): If the defender is playing very loose at five yards or more, the receiver simply sells deep and runs a regular route. This technique also works if the defender aligns closer and backpedals before or at the snap.

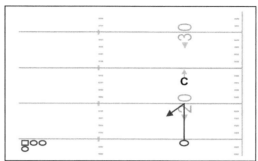

Figure 7-38. Stop route option #5: Loose man head-up leverage

Slant Versus Loose Man

Option #1—Loose Man (Inside): Since this route is an inside breaking route and the defender is playing with inside leverage, the receiver runs at the defender's framework to square him up and to create separation at the break. At depth, he makes a slant break with a head-and-shoulder fake to the outside.

Option #2—Loose Man (Inside): The receiver takes two steps at the defender's inside shoulder and two quick steps outside to turn his hips. He then cuts across the defender's face to the slant route. The receiver must have quick feet to execute this move.

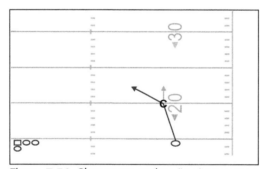

Figure 7-39. Slant route option #1: Loose man inside leverage

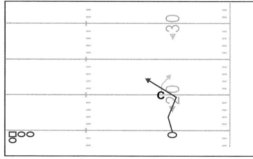

Figure 7-40. Slant route option #2: Loose man inside leverage

Option #3—Loose Man (Head-Up): If the defender sits at four to five yards, the receiver releases vertical at the defender, runs his regular route, and sells deep with a head fake at the break. He uses the push-him-by technique at the breakpoint if needed.

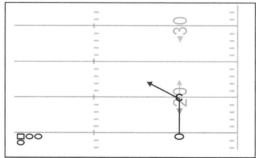

Figure 7-41. Slant route option #3: Loose man head-up leverage

Option #4—Loose Man (Head-Up): If the defender is playing very loose at five yards or more, the receiver simply sells deep and runs a regular route. This technique also works if the defender aligns closer and backpedals before or at the snap. The receiver should be untouched while running this route.

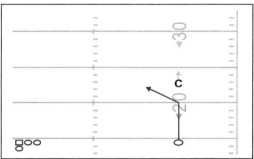

Figure 7-42. Slant route option #4: Loose man head-up leverage

Curl Versus Loose Man

Option #1—Loose Man (Inside): The receiver releases at the defender and slips by him on the inside (e.g., dip-and-rip). The receiver then uses body lean to get back on the stem and to avoid giving up ground inside. At the breakpoint, he makes a cut and comes back to the football.

Option #2—Loose Man (Inside): If the defender's technique does not allow an inside release, the receiver pushes vertical and keeps the defender on his inside hip. He uses the push-him-by technique at the breakpoint to get open, and he then comes back to the football.

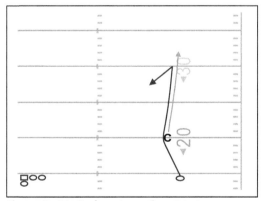

Figure 7-43. Curl route option #1: Loose man inside leverage

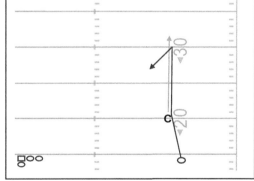

Figure 7-44. Curl route option #2: Loose man inside leverage

Option #3 – Loose Man (Head-Up): The receiver releases at the defender and slips by him on the inside (e.g., dip-and-rip). The receiver then uses body lean to get back on the stem, makes the break, and comes back to the football.

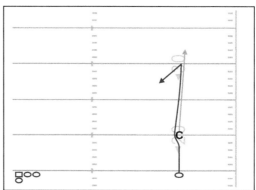

Figure 7-45. Curl route option #3: Loose man head-up leverage

Square-In Versus Loose Man

Option #1—Loose Man (Inside): The receiver releases at the defender and slips by him on the inside (e.g., dip-and-rip). The receiver then uses body lean to get back on the stem and to avoid giving up ground inside. At the breakpoint, he makes his inside cut with either a head bob or head-and-shoulder fake and runs straight across the field.

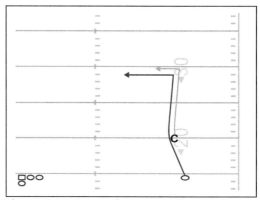

Figure 7-46. Square-in route option #1: Loose man inside leverage

Option #2—Loose Man (Inside): If the defender's technique does not allow an inside release, the receiver pushes vertical and keeps the defender on his inside hip. He uses the push-him-by technique at the breakpoint to get open and runs straight across the field.

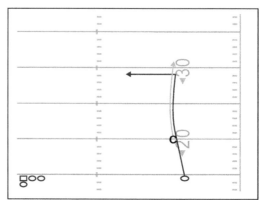

Figure 7-47. Square-in route option #2: Loose man inside leverage

Option #3—Loose Man (Head-Up): The receiver releases at the defender and slips by him on the inside (e.g., dip-and-rip). He then uses body lean to the outside to get back on the stem of the route before the breakpoint and then runs straight across the field.

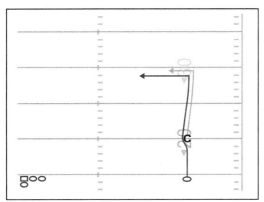

Figure 7-48. Square-in route option #3: Loose man head-up leverage

Dig (Post Stem) Versus Loose Man

Option #1—Loose Man (Inside): The receiver releases at the defender and slips by him on the inside (e.g., dip-and-rip). The receiver then uses body lean to get back on the stem and to avoid giving up ground inside. At the first breakpoint, he makes a post break. At the second breakpoint, he makes the cut to the dig route with an optional head bob to continue selling the post, and then proceeds straight across the field.

Option #2—Loose Man (Inside): If the defender's technique does not allow an inside release, the receiver runs at the defender and keeps him on his hip as he makes the break to the post. He sells the deep post route so that the defender is running full speed to cover the post. At the second breakpoint, he uses the push-him-by technique if needed and proceeds straight across the field.

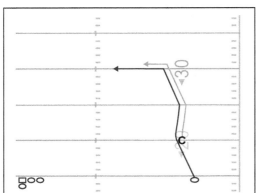

Figure 7-49. Dig route option #1: Loose man inside leverage

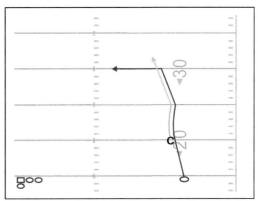

Figure 7-50. Dig route option #2: Loose man inside leverage

Option #3—Loose Man (Head-Up): The receiver releases at the defender and slips by him on the inside. Using body lean, the receiver keeps the defender on his outside hip and makes a post break at the first breakpoint. At the second breakpoint, he makes the cut to the dig route with an optional head bob to the post and proceeds straight across the field.

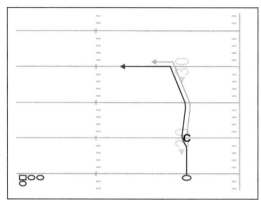

Figure 7-51. Dig route option #3: Loose man head-up leverage

Post Versus Loose Man

Option #1—Loose Man (Inside): The receiver squares up the defender, slips him on the inside (e.g., dip-and-rip), and gets back on the stem using body lean. At the breakpoint, he gives an outside head-and-shoulder fake.

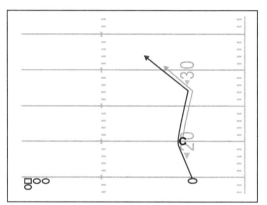

Figure 7-52. Post route option #1: Loose man inside leverage

Option #2—Loose Man (Inside): If the defender's technique does not allow an inside release, the receiver runs toward his outside shoulder. During the stem, he uses weave technique to the outside to sell the corner route and lure the defender to his outside hip. He makes a head-and-shoulder fake at the breakpoint.

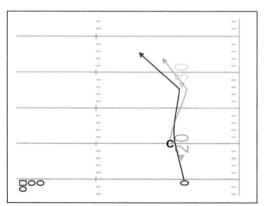

Figure 7-53. Post route option #2: Loose man inside leverage

Option #3—Loose Man (Head-Up): The receiver releases at the defender's outside shoulder to turn the defender's hips to the outside and get him running upfield. The receiver slips him on the inside and runs the route with a head-and-shoulder fake to the outside at the breakpoint.

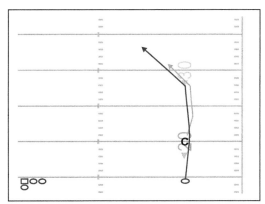

Figure 7-54. Post route option #3: Loose man head-up leverage

Out Versus Loose Man

Option #1—Loose Man (Inside): The receiver runs at the defender's outside shoulder and pushes vertical upfield while keeping the defender on his inside hip—using body lean if warranted. He then makes a square cut with a head-and-shoulder fake and runs flat toward the sideline.

Option #2—Loose Man (Head-Up): The receiver releases at the defender. He slips him on the outside (e.g., dip-and-rip) and works back to the stem by using body lean if contact continues. He then makes a square cut with a head-and-shoulder fake and runs flat toward the sideline.

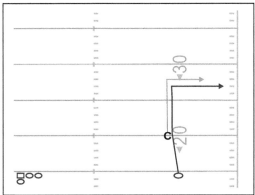

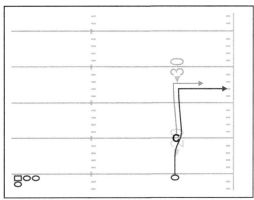

Figure 7-55. Out route option #1: Loose man inside leverage

Figure 7-56. Out route option #2: Loose man head-up leverage

Fade Versus Loose Man

Option #1—Loose Man (Inside): The receiver runs at the defender's outside shoulder to create more room to catch the ball on the sideline. He uses body lean to the inside, beats the defender deep, and makes a fade adjustment to the ball.

Option #2—Loose Man (Head-Up): The receiver releases at the defender, slips by on the outside (e.g., dip-and-rip), gets back on the stem, and makes a fade adjustment to the ball.

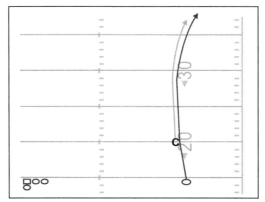

Figure 7-57. Fade route option #1: Loose man inside leverage

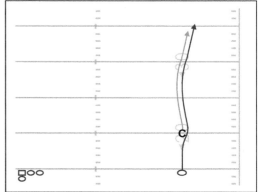

Figure 7-58. Fade route option #2: Loose man head-up leverage

Comeback Versus Loose Man

Option #1—Loose Man (Inside): The receiver runs at the defender's outside shoulder, slips him on the outside, uses body lean to the inside, and sells deep. He may briefly look to the inside (fade fake) before the breakpoint. He comes back toward the sideline to catch the ball.

Option #2—Loose Man (Head-Up): The receiver releases at the defender to avoid giving up too much ground to the outside. He then slips him on the outside (e.g., dip-and-rip), gets back on the stem, and sells deep. He may briefly look to the inside at the breakpoint (fade fake) and comes back to catch the ball on the sideline.

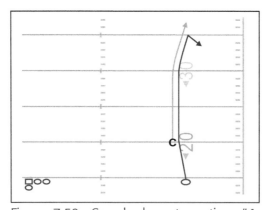

Figure 7-59. Comeback route option #1: Loose man inside leverage

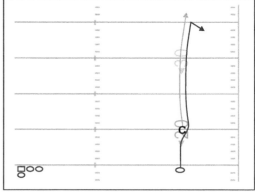

Figure 7-60. Comeback route option #2: Loose man head-up leverage

ZONE

The concept behind zone coverages is to break the field into several areas or zones that specific defenders have the responsibility of protecting. Defenders cover their area and attack any offensive player in their zone. The defensive side of the line of scrimmage is divided into three levels of zones:

- The first level (underneath)
- The second level (middle)
- The third level (deep)

The zones are divided and can be labeled as shown in Figures 7-61 through 7-65. The third level contains the deep zones. The figures show how the deep zones can be divided based on the coverage. The coverages—cover zero (pure man), cover 1 (man free), cover 2, cover 3, cover 4—get their names simply based on the number of defenders in the deep portion of the field.

Coverage	Number of Deep Defenders
Cover zero	zero
Cover 1	one (one safety)
Cover 2	two (two safeties)
Cover 3	three (one safety, two corners)
Cover 4	four (two safeties, two corners)

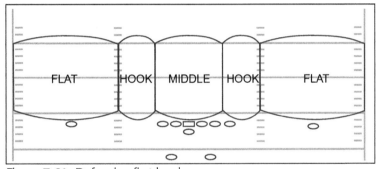

Figure 7-61. Defensive first-level zones

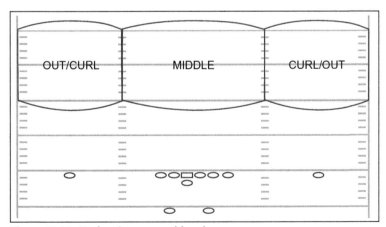

Figure 7-62. Defensive second-level zones

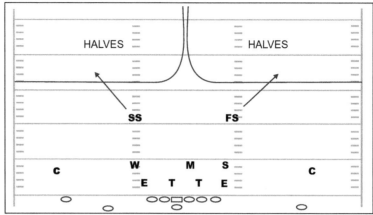

Figure 7-63. Defensive third-level zones—cover 2: deep half zones "halves"

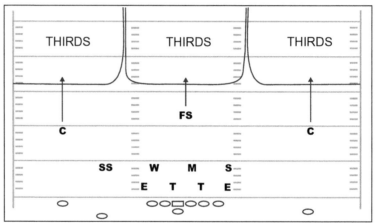

Figure 7-64. Defensive third-level zones—cover 3: deep third zones "thirds"

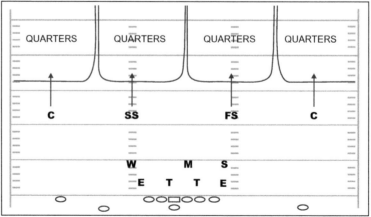

Figure 7-65. Defensive third-level zones—cover 4: deep quarter zones "quarters"

This section analyzes each type of coverage and identifies route packages that exploit the weaknesses of that coverage.

- A general principle for defeating zone coverages is to send two or more receivers into one defender's zone to make him pick which one to cover. The ball goes to the uncovered receiver.

- Another way to defeat zone coverages is to send a receiver to a part of the field where the defender has a large area to cover (e.g., a stop route in the linebacker's flat zone against cover 3).

- Against zone coverages, plays may be designed to get the receivers in a window between zones. The receivers should wait in this window for the pass, as opposed to continuing to run full speed and directly into the arms of a defender, who is lurking in the next zone.

- Versus zone coverages, the receiver has less need to stem, weave, and fake during the route because the splashdown is an open window in the zone, and often the defender is guarding his area and is not right on the receiver. Therefore, the route can often be run plain.

COVER 2

The basic rules of cover 2 are:

- Safeties protect the deep halves of the field with an emphasis on not getting beat down the sideline.

- Outside linebackers protect the hook and curl zones.

- Middle or inside linebackers protect the hook and middle zones.

- Cornerbacks have run responsibility first, and on pass plays protect the flat zones.

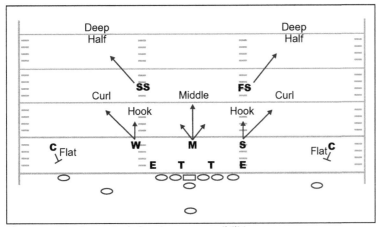

Figure 7-66. Cover-2 defensive responsibilities

o   If a receiver enters a cornerback's zone and runs past a depth of 10 yards, the cornerback lets that receiver go on and enter the safety's zone while the cornerback checks for an additional receiver coming into the flat. If a new receiver is there, he covers him. If no one else is penetrating his zone, the cornerback continues to cover the initial receiver with a trail technique as he progresses downfield. Therefore, many cover-2 route packages are predicated on one route stopping in the flat area to hold the cornerback there.

○   In cover-2 press, the cornerbacks may jam the receivers at the line of scrimmage with the intent of disrupting their routes and funneling them inside. Cornerbacks are taught to have their eyes on the outside receiver as well as on the inside receiver at the same time while also reading the backfield. In order for them to accomplish this task, they generally align with outside leverage and are often cocked toward the quarterback. Unlike in man coverage, they must keep all possible receivers on their side in full view.

Weaknesses: The middle of the field (between the two safeties) and the sideline area between the cornerback's zone and the deep safety

How to Recognize Cover 2

Keys that the coverage is cover 2 include:

*   Two safeties are aligned on or near the hash marks, and usually around 12 yards deep.
*   The cornerbacks are typically at a depth of six yards or less, and are aligned with outside leverage and with their body cocked toward the formation to view both the quarterback and receiver(s). They usually either initiate contact and/or sit at depth instead of backpedaling.

COVER 3

The basic rules of cover 3 are:

*   The free safety covers the deep middle third of the field with emphasis on not getting beat deep.
*   Cornerbacks cover the deep third of the field on their side with emphasis on not getting beat deep.
*   The strong safety and outside linebacker are normally run defenders first while covering the curl/flat area on their side for passes.
*   The inside linebackers cover the hook and middle zones.

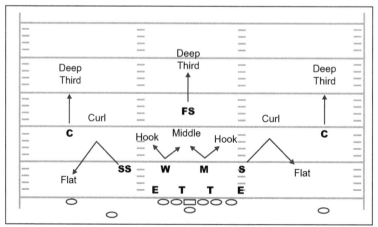

Figure 7-67. Cover-3 defensive responsibilities

Weaknesses: The flat, hook, curl, and middle zones. (It is hard for slower linebacker types to cover all these areas.) Because cover 3 has three deep defenders, it generally protects well against the long ball but allows the offense to get short and medium gains.

How to Recognize Cover 3

Keys that the coverage is cover 3 include:

- One safety is in the middle of the field, and he is usually around 12 yards deep.
- The cornerbacks are typically head-up or with slight outside leverage and at six yards or more. They are often cocked to view both the receiver and the quarterback, and they bail at the snap in an effort not to get beat deep.

COVER 4

The basic rules of cover 4 are:

- Safeties play the run first and pass second and are responsible for covering the curl zones and deep middle quarters of the field.
- Cornerbacks protect the deep outside quarters of the field with emphasis on not getting beat deep.
- Outside linebackers are responsible for the flats.
- The middle linebacker is responsible for the middle of the field.

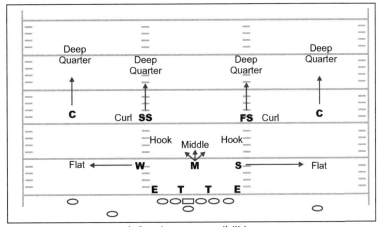

Figure 7-68. Cover-4 defensive responsibilities

Weaknesses: The flats (because it's hard for slow linebackers to get out to the flats) and the middle of the field underneath the deep coverage (because this area of the field is very large and therefore difficult for the middle linebacker to cover). Some programs use cover 4 as a type of prevent defense where the safeties and cornerbacks play even deeper. In this situation, the first- and second-level zones are even more vulnerable.

How to Recognize Cover 4

Keys that the coverage is cover 4 include:

- Two safeties are on or near the hash marks, and usually around 10 to 12 yards deep.

- The cornerbacks are often aligned head-up or with slight outside leverage and close to the depth of the safeties. They bail at the snap in an effort not to get beat deep.

ROUTE ADJUSTMENTS VERSUS ZONE

Stop Versus Zone

Option #1—Cover 2: The cornerback sits in the flat. The receiver pushes vertical and runs the route. Unless the cornerback blows the coverage, the receiver will not get the ball in this situation because the cornerback, as the flat defender, is sitting on the stop route. The receiver's duty is thus to occupy the cornerback to free up another receiver. Some offenses have an automatic conversion of the stop route to a fade, slant, or five-yard in route versus cover 2.

Option #2—Cover 3: The receiver runs a plain route and sells deep. The cornerback backpedals since his responsibility is the deep thirds, and the receiver can easily run the route underneath him.

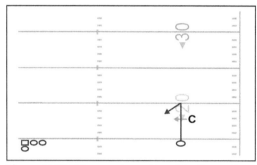

Figure 7-69. Stop route option #1: Cover 2

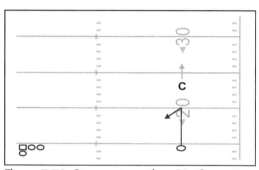

Figure 7-70. Stop route option #2: Cover 3

Option #3—Cover 4: The receiver runs a plain route and sells deep. The cornerback backpedals since his responsibility is the deep quarters, and the receiver can easily run the route underneath him.

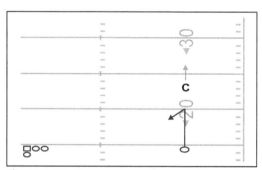

Figure 7-71. Stop route option #3: Cover 4

Slant Versus Zone

Option #1—Cover 2: The cornerback sits in the flat. The receiver pushes vertical and runs the route with a head-and-shoulder fake to the outside. The cornerback ends up in trail technique.

Option #2—Cover 3: The cornerback backpedals. The receiver runs a basic route underneath the coverage.

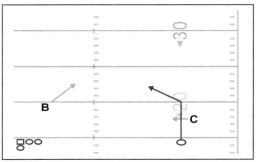
Figure 7-72. Slant route option #1: Cover 2

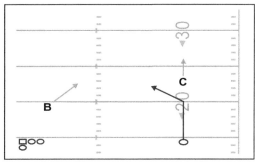
Figure 7-73. Slant route option #2: Cover 3

Option #3—Cover 4: The cornerback backpedals. The receiver runs a basic route underneath the coverage. He should keep in mind that the near safety will run up to make the play, so the receiver should be ready to make a move immediately after the catch.

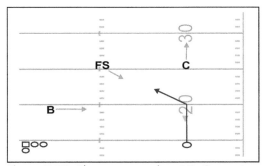
Figure 7-74. Slant route option #3: Cover 4

Curl Versus Zone

Option #1—Cover 2: The cornerback sits in the flat. The receiver pushes vertical and runs the route. After the break, he works to get open in a window behind the linebacker(s) by either retracing his footsteps back down the stem of his route, working back toward the quarterback, or working flat toward the middle of the field.

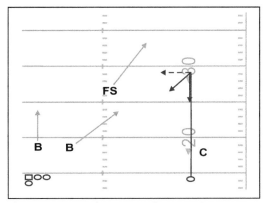
Figure 7-75. Curl route option #1: Cover 2

Option #2—Cover 3: The cornerback backpedals. The receiver runs the route and, at the breakpoint, reads the linebacker(s) to find the open window. He will most likely turn and work back toward the quarterback or possibly move toward the middle of the field on a flat path.

Option #3—Cover 4: The cornerback backpedals. The receiver runs the route and, at the breakpoint, reads the near safety and linebacker to find the open window. He most likely will turn and work back toward the quarterback or possibly move toward the middle of the field on a flat path.

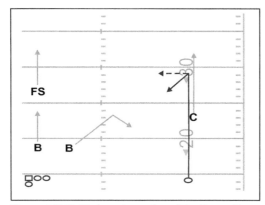

Figure 7-76. Curl route option #2: Cover 3

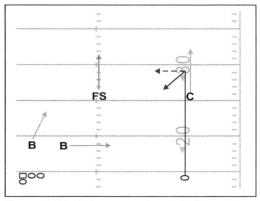

Figure 7-77. Curl route option #3: Cover 4

Square-In Versus Zone

Option #1—Cover 2: The cornerback sits in the flat. The receiver releases inside, pushes vertical, and runs the route. After the break, he expects the ball in a window between the linebackers toward the middle of the field.

Option #2—Cover 3: The cornerback bails. The receiver runs a normal square-in route. The ball should be thrown in a window between the linebackers.

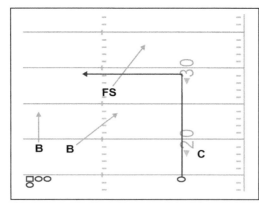

Figure 7-78. Square-in route option #1: Cover 2

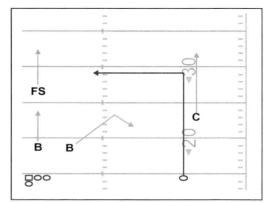

Figure 7-79. Square-in route option #2: Cover 3

Option #3—Cover 4: The cornerback bails. The receiver runs a normal square-in route. He should expect the ball quickly after his break, as a safety is in the near middle quarter of the field.

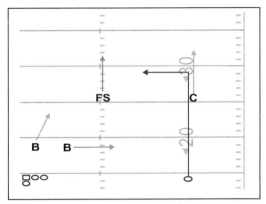

Figure 7-80. Square-in route option #3: Cover 4

Dig (Post Stem) Versus Zone

Option #1—Cover 2: The cornerback sits in the flat and allows an inside release. The receiver runs a plain route, makes a good head-bob fake to sell the post to the safety, and breaks flat to the middle of the field. After the break, he expects the ball in a window between the linebackers toward the middle of the field.

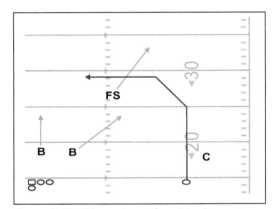

Figure 7-81. Dig route option #1: Cover 2

Option #2—Cover 3: The cornerback bails. The receiver runs a regular route, sells the deep post, and expects the ball in the open window between the linebackers.

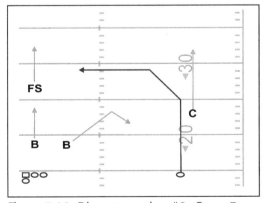

Figure 7-82. Dig route option #2: Cover 3

Option #3—Cover 4: The cornerback bails. The receiver runs a normal route, sells the deep post, and expects the ball in the middle of the field between the safeties.

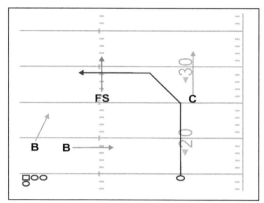

Figure 7-83. Dig route option #3: Cover 4

Post Versus Zone

Option #1—Cover 2: The cornerback sits in the flat. The receiver pushes vertical and runs the regular route. He expects the ball in the middle of the field between the two safeties.

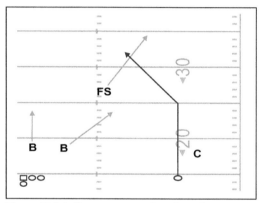

Figure 7-84. Post route option #1: Cover 2

Option #2—Cover 3: Because of the location of the free safety in the middle of the field, the route should be adjusted to a skinny post. The receiver runs a vertical stem at the backpedaling cornerback and makes the break with the near upright as the aiming point.

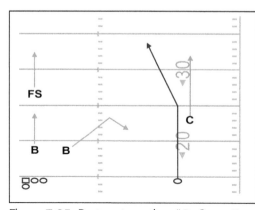

Figure 7-85. Post route option #2: Cover 3

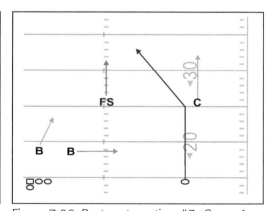

Figure 7-86. Post route option #3: Cover 4

Option #3—Cover 4: The objective versus cover 4 is to get behind the near safety who is sitting on the run first. The receiver therefore runs a vertical stem at the cornerback who is bailing and breaks to the post.

Out Versus Zone

Option #1—Cover 2: With the cornerback staying in the flat, the receiver releases vertical and runs a regular route. If the cornerback does trail on the hip of the receiver, the receiver makes a good head-bob fake to the deep route and if necessary uses the push-him-by technique at the breakpoint.

Option #2—Cover 3: The receiver releases vertical, sells the deep route so that the cornerback continues to bail to the deep threat, and makes the square cut at the breakpoint.

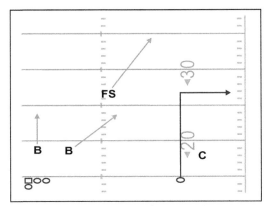
Figure 7-87. Out route option #1: Cover 2

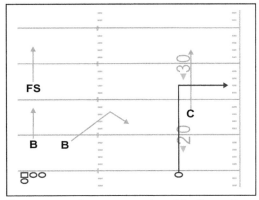
Figure 7-88. Out route option #2: Cover 3

Option #3—Cover 4: The receiver releases vertical, sells the deep route so that the cornerback continues to bail to the deep threat, and makes the square cut at the breakpoint.

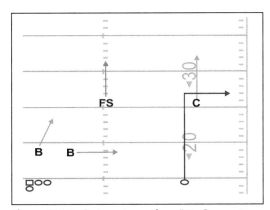
Figure 7-89. Out route option #3: Cover 4

Fade Versus Zone

Option #1—Cover 2: The receiver fights for an outside release (e.g., dip-and-rip). Once he is beyond the cornerback who typically sits in the flat, the receiver turns his head and looks for the ball. Since the window for the catch is behind the cornerback and in front of the safety near the sideline, the receiver does not have to worry about getting back on the stem. This scenario is the only exception to the five-yard highway rule.

Option #2—Cover 2: Versus cover 2, some offenses encourage an inside release to save time. Once beyond the cornerback in the flat, the receiver adjusts the route to bend to the open window near the sideline.

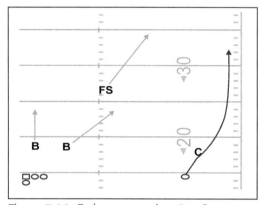 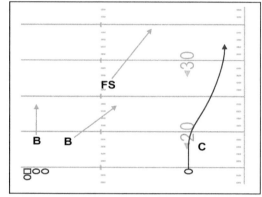

Figure 7-90. Fade route option #1: Cover 2   Figure 7-91. Fade route option #2: Cover 2

Option #3—Cover 3: The receiver runs a regular route. However, the cornerback's cushion and bail may preclude the receiver from getting past him and getting the ball. Therefore, versus cover 3, this route should be in a package that is designed to get the ball in someone else's hands.

Option #4—Cover 4: The receiver runs a normal route. However, the cornerback's cushion and bail may preclude the receiver from getting past him and getting the ball. Therefore versus cover 4, this route should be in a package that is designed to get the ball in someone else's hands.

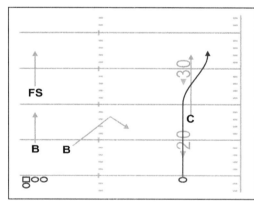 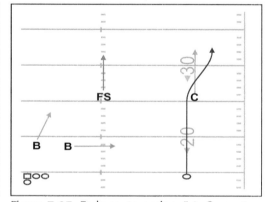

Figure 7-92. Fade route option #3: Cover 3   Figure 7-93. Fade route option #4: Cover 4

Comeback Versus Zone

Option #1—Cover 2: The receiver takes whatever release the cornerback gives—generally to the inside. The receiver does not need to waste time trying for an outside release. The receiver sells deep, makes a cut at the breakpoint, and comes back to the ball on the sideline and away from the safety.

Option #2—Cover 3: The receiver runs his normal route, sells deep, and makes the cut at the breakpoint with a head bob to push the cornerback deeper.

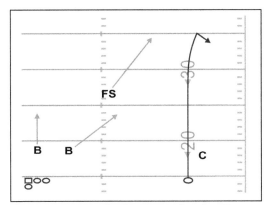
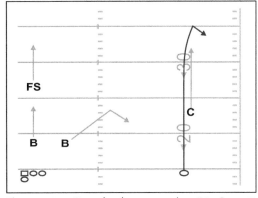

Figure 7-94. Comeback route option #1: Cover 2   Figure 7-95. Comeback route option #2: Cover 3

Option #3—Cover 4: The receiver runs his normal route, sells deep, and makes the cut at the breakpoint with a head bob to push the cornerback deeper.

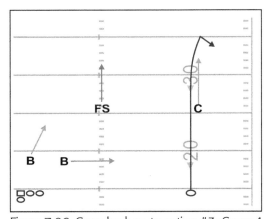

Figure 7-96. Comeback route option #3: Cover 4

THE WIDE BLOCKER

Chapter Eight

A wide receiver has two jobs. One of the receiver's jobs is catching the football, scoring a touchdown, getting his name in the paper, and becoming rich and famous. The other job—blocking—is much less glamorous. For this reason, and perhaps because of the physicality involved, receivers often disdain blocking.

However, effective receiver blocking significantly helps the offense in moving the ball downfield and scoring points. A good downfield block by a receiver can turn a five-yard run or pass into a 50-yard touchdown. Or looking at it from the flipside, notice how many times the tackle is made by a defender who has escaped a receiver's block. Moreover, when you compare the number of blocks by and the number of passes to one receiver in a typical game, the results would suggest that receivers should be called wide blockers, and not wide receivers. Receivers need to be blockers first.

Along with receivers, coaches are sometimes mesmerized by the glamorous part of the job—the passing game. They also tend to think that because blocking is largely "want to" and "heart," receivers can automatically rise to the occasion during a game. Because of the focus on catching, and because many coaches do not view blocking as a skill learned through detailed explanation of technique and through multiple reps, blocking by wide receivers is not sufficiently practiced in many programs. At least one blocking drill should be included in the individual receiver practice time every day. It should also be included in pre-game warm-ups so that receivers go into a game with already having had the feel of light contact.

Running the Defender Off

The easiest block to make is not a physical block at all. The receiver simply runs deep and keeps the defender with him to take the defender out of the play. This technique is currently popular due to the emphasis on passing offenses. The defender is primed to expect a pass and thus easily seduced into believing the receiver is going deep.

However, running the defender off is only effective when the defender is in man-to-man coverage and has his eyes fixed on the receiver. The receiver must take an outside release to make sure the defender's back is to the play. If the defender's eyes are not completely fixed on the receiver, he will be able to see the backfield, realize it is a running play, and act accordingly. Thus, running the defender off does not work in zone coverages or in loose man coverage.

When the receiver chooses to run the man-to-man defender off, the receiver must develop a feel for the location of the defender as they run together down the field. At some point, the defender may recognize that it is a run play and drop off from pursuing the receiver to make a play on the ballcarrier. The receiver must instinctively recognize this situation and react immediately as he starts to lose the defender. He needs to quickly break down and block the defender. A weakness of this technique is that by the time the receiver realizes the defender is no longer with him, it may be too late to execute an effective block, and the defender may run uncontested to the ballcarrier.

Stalk Block

The classic block for receivers is the stalk block. It is used the vast majority of times a receiver is called upon to block. In this block, the receiver's objective is to stay between the defender and the ballcarrier. The receiver must not let the defender get by him. When the block is successful, it allows the ballcarrier to cut in the optimal direction upfield off the block.

Burst Off the Line

In a stalk block, a receiver bursts off the line and runs in the direction of the defender he is going to block. One of the keys to an effective stalk block is for the receiver not to hint that a running play is coming by leaving the line of scrimmage in a lackadaisical manner. When looking at high school—and even college—game films, coaches, opponents, and (sadly) sometimes even casual observers can often tell whether the play is a run or a pass based on how a receiver leaves the line. To give your offense full advantage on each play, receivers must be trained (and held accountable) to burst off the line of scrimmage with the same aggressive manner on every play whether it is a run or a pass. Do not let your receivers help the defense by being lazy, arrogant, or undisciplined in this aspect of the game.

The Approach

After bursting off the line, the receiver takes an angle that puts him in a position between the ballcarrier and the defender to execute an effective stalk block. This position shields the ballcarrier from the defender. As the defender recognizes the run (stops his backpedal), the receiver throttles down from his full sprint at five yards from the defender and assumes a breakdown position. If the receiver gets too close to the defender before breaking down, he will enable the defender to juke past the receiver and get to the ballcarrier. The receiver therefore needs to maintain this cushion and not overpursue (i.e., go past the point where the receiver can stay in front of and squared up on the defender).

Figure 8-1. Proper cushion on a stalk block

During the breakdown, the receiver needs to square up the defender and be fully under control. In this coiled breakdown position, his back is straight, his knees are bent, his hips are down (like a defender in basketball), his feet are slightly wider than shoulder-width and angled slightly outside for stability, and he is on the balls of his feet. The receiver now maintains a two- to three-yard cushion and shadows the defender by mirroring his movements by moving laterally back and forth with him.

Figure 8-2. Breakdown during the stalk block

As the defender moves to make a play on the ballcarrier, the cushion will start to close. However, the receiver should maintain an arm's length distance from the defender. This distance ensures the receiver is close enough to the defender so that he does not have to lunge to make contact, but far enough away to be able to read the defender and move laterally. It is important for the receiver to keep moving his feet laterally and stay squared up on the defender. If the receiver tries to block the defender from the side, the defender can sprint by him. The receiver should never attack by overextending, lunging, or diving at the defender; he should always wait for the defender to come to him so as not to get juked.

Eyes

The key to reading a defender's movements pre-contact is to watch his belt buckle, which is another reason not to be too close before contact is initiated. However, once contact is made, the receiver should read the defender's eyes as he focuses on the ballcarrier. The defender's eyes tip off the direction he is going to move. The defender can juke with his head and shoulders just like a receiver, but the belt buckle and the eyes won't lie.

The most important point about the eyes, however, and probably the most important point in this book, is to *see what you hit*. The receiver must keep his head up in order to be successful in his block, but more importantly to prevent serious injury. This point is so important point that some NFL teams have a sign posted to this effect in their locker rooms.

Feet

To make a successful stalk block, it is important for the receiver to keep his feet moving (quick feet!) and mirror the footwork of the defender. If the receiver lets up on this motion for even a second, the defender can get by him. This type of footwork is very similar to man-to-man defense in basketball.

Again, it is imperative during a stalk block that the receiver stays low, keeps his weight on the balls of his feet, and keeps his feet slightly wider than shoulder-width apart. If he does not, he will not be able to move laterally quickly enough to keep up with the defender, or he may get tipped over by the defender bull-rushing through him.

Hands and Arms

Contact ensues when the receiver is at arm's length from the defender, and the defender makes his move to the ballcarrier. The receiver makes the block by vigorously extending his arms, hitting the defender's chest with his hands, and locking his elbows. That is, the receiver punches the defender in the chest with both his arms fully extended at the elbows. This motion is called shooting the hands to the chest of the defender. The receiver comes at the defender from low to high. He should hit the defender with the palms of his hands. Although some coaches teach to block with the fingers pointing straight up, the preferred position is with the thumbs up, which is important for three reasons:

- The punch has more power.
- It is easier to get a hold of the defender's shoulder pads.
- The receiver is less likely to break a finger.

It is important for the receiver to make contact with his hands on the chest of the defender. He should not initiate contact on the defender's arm or outside shoulder area, as doing so will result in a holding call. A holding penalty may also result if the official sees the receiver pull the jersey of the defender in any way.

Figure 8-3. Error: holding during a stalk block

The receiver can finish the block in four ways. The best receivers alternate these techniques so that the defender does not know what to expect on any given play.

- The receiver may choose to grab the underside of the defender's shoulder pads, lock his arms out, and steer the defender. In the grab-and-steer method, it is especially important to coach the receiver not to pull the defender's jersey away from his body.

- The receiver may wish to punch and reload. The receiver punches (shoots his hands straight at the defender's chest) and reloads rhythmically as he mirrors the defender's footwork by taking sideways shuffle steps. It is important that the receiver keep a good athletic position and stay on the balls of his feet throughout the entire block. The receiver must hold the block long enough to allow the ballcarrier to get upfield.

- The receiver may wish to punch and recoil. He delivers a vigorous blow to the defender, with the force of the blow pushing the receiver off the defender for up to five yards. This move is not made rhythmically with the shuffling footwork. It is one severe blow after which the receiver must gather himself (regain balance and position), resume his mirroring footwork, and repeat the punch and recoil movements. The advantage of this method is that after the blow it gets the receiver aligned far enough away from the defender that the receiver can easily read the defender's movements, and the receiver is therefore less likely to get juked. It also has the advantage of leaving the defender not knowing what hit him.

- The receiver may also take the defender where he wants to go. In other words, the receiver takes advantage of the defender's momentum to help push him in the direction the defender is trying to go, and the running back makes his cut accordingly. As discussed in the head section of this chapter, the receiver needs to position his helmet on the breastplate of the defender's shoulder pads. (Again, for safety, the receiver needs to be sure to have his head and eyes up to see what he's making contact with.) Doing so helps the receiver push the defender in the direction he wants to go and avoids a blocking in the back or holding penalty. The hand position is one hand on the front of the defender and one on his hip (similar to a tight end's down block). A danger is that the official may look up and see slipped hands (i.e., the receiver's hands have moved to the defender's shoulders or outer arms), and the referee calls holding without having seen the location of the initial contact that makes the entire scenario legal. The difference between this block and other blocks is that the running back must make his cut off the block as opposed to running to a pre-designated area he knows the receiver will open up for him. Taking a defender

Figure 8-4. Grab-and-steer on a stalk block

where he wants to go is one technique a smaller receiver can use to effectively block a bigger defender. The receiver is not fighting the larger defender's strength, but rather is using the defender's own momentum as a weapon against him.

Figure 8-5. Punch and reload with knees bent and a straight back

Body

As he blocks, the receiver must remember the classic football rule: the low man wins. If he has his knees flexed, his body in coiled athletic position, stays low, and has quick feet, even a small receiver can successfully block a larger defender. It is easy to say, "Stay lower than you opponent," but it takes lots of reps to get your receivers to do so consistently.

Head

The receiver needs to think about the position of his head during the block. The helmet must always be in front of the defender's shoulder pads or a penalty may be called. However, in order to establish a favorable leverage position between the defender and the ballcarrier during contact, the receiver's helmet should be to the right or left side of the defender's framework. The receiver puts his helmet to the opposite side from the direction the receiver is trying to move the defender. That is, when moving the defender to the inside, the receiver's helmet is on the outside of the defender's body.

Besides knowing where to position the helmet, the receivers need to use what's in it—the mind. In order to be effective blockers, receivers need to know where the running play is going—at a minimum, to their side or away and outside versus inside run. The receiver needs to know the objective of the play, so he can create a situation that gives the running back the best chance to cut effectively and advance more rapidly. Accordingly, a receiver must focus on the angle of his block:

- Typically, on the playside, the receiver is blocking a defender who is aligned relatively near him. With stalk blocks, it is generally important to give the running back an option for his upfield cut. However, in some systems the receiver may be taught to attack half the body of the defender in order to give the running back the best running path. For example, a receiver might attack the inside shoulder of a defender to seal him outside to allow the running back to run through the alley on a sweep play.

- On the backside, the receiver's target will often be a safety, who is aligned significantly inside of him and may be quite deep as well (12 yards). The receiver must take a cutoff angle while running to this safety. That is, the receiver must factor in what the safety is reading in the play and his resulting angle of pursuit. Players, especially in high school, often have trouble cutting the defenders off at the pass. Instead, they incorrectly make their aiming point the area of the safety at the start of the play. The receiver then ends up chasing the backside of his prey across the field.

Heart

Besides the fundamentals discussed previously, stalk blocking really comes down to heart—courage, determination, and persistence. Receivers must have the attitude of "no way is this defender going to get away from me to make the tackle." (Think: Jerry Rice.)

Receivers at all levels of football tend to stop blocking sooner than they should. Few things are as humiliating as when the backside defender gets off of a receiver's block and stops what would otherwise be a touchdown run. Therefore, it is extremely important that all blocking drills be practiced not just to the whistle, but through the whistle. It is really useful to make it a slow whistle so that athletes learn to stay on the block for an exaggerated length of time.

To further underscore the importance of aggressive receiver blocking, coaches can use the concept of RBIs (runs batted in) as part of the weekly grading of receivers (Appendix F). In this grading system, RBIs are blocks that spring runs of over 15 yards. This approach emphasizes to the receivers in a concrete way the importance of blocking. Use the loaf category of the grading sheet for negative points for receivers who do not block aggressively or don't burst off the line on blocking plays.

You can also have fun with the song "Every Breath You Take" ("Every move you make, I'll be watching you"), by The Police. Receivers want to be watched and admired, so tell them this tune is your theme song for blocking. And, when they know their coach is watching their blocking as intently as their route running and catching, the receivers tend to block more aggressively and longer than when they think their coach doesn't consider blocking a priority or just assumes it will get done.

Drive Block

Another kind of block that can be effectively used by a wide receiver is the drive block. This block is used primarily by tight ends and linemen, but it makes a great change-up when used by a receiver on a cornerback. It is an attacking type of block, whereas the stalk block is more reactive. The basic technique is the same as for a stalk block (burst off the line, approach, eyes, feet, body, head, and heart) until the point when the defender makes a move on the ballcarrier. The receiver is then coiled in his breakdown position, and two to three yards away from the defender. When the defender starts to make a move on the ballcarrier, the receiver attacks the defender by rapidly closing the gap between them and executes the drive block, as follows:

- Upon contact, the receiver punches up with his arms into the chest of the opponent, thrusts upward, and drives through with energy coming from his power center. This use of the power center and thrusting motion is similar to tackling technique.

- The receiver locks onto the defender by grabbing the chest plate of the defender's shoulder pads with the thumbs up.

- The receiver keeps his legs moving and drives (pushes) the defender out of the way of the play. Continuing to keep the feet moving is the key to a successful drive block.

Figure 8-6. Drive block

With the drive block, it is easy to overextend. Therefore, the receiver must not let his back become too horizontal, with his hips pushed out, and his head down during the block.

Figure 8-7. Error: Overextension on a drive block

Cut Block

A cut block is a legal block below the waist, which must be executed from the front of the defender. In executing a cut block, the receiver aims at and throws his shoulder to the opposite thigh of the defender (e.g., the receiver's right shoulder drives at the defender's right thigh). It is important to teach receivers to aim for the thigh. If they aim for the knee, two bad things may happen. By aiming at the knee, the receiver may actually hit the defender only at ankle height, which allows the defender to easily hop over him to make a play on the ballcarrier. More importantly, the defender's knee may be blown out.

As the receiver's shoulder makes contact with the defender's thigh, the receiver rolls into the defender. At higher levels of football, receivers are sometimes taught to aim at the defender's crotch with a flexed arm and clenched fist as an added deterrent. As the receiver rolls into the defender, he must keep rolling and not just stop his block after the initial blow. Otherwise, the defender can easily jump over the receiver and escape him. One technique that helps counter this escape is for the receiver to keep his knees up and flexed during the roll(s).

A cut block is used:

- When the defender is about to escape a stalk block and make a play on the ballcarrier.

- When a defender consistently plays the run and tries to bull-rush through the receiver to the ball.

- To gain respect. If a receiver throws a cut block at a defender early in a game, he will treat the receiver with more respect (i.e., be somewhat afraid of him) for the rest of the game.

- As a change-up. A cut block keeps the defender off balance by not letting him stay in the comfort zone of routine stalk blocks.

Figure 8-8. Body position on a cut block

Figure 8-9. The finish of the cut block

The two ways to enter a cut block are as follows. One is to enter directly from running. The other is to move from a stalk block into the cut block. To successfully execute a cut block from a stalk-block position, the receiver must be an arm's length away (or less) from the defender. Otherwise, the receiver will end up taking a dive, rolling on the ground, and allowing the defender to easily jump or hop over him. Also, it is important for the receiver to execute the cut block only when the defender is about to escape or when the ballcarrier is nearby. If the receiver cuts too early, the defender may recover and make the play.

Cut blocking is very difficult to practice live because of the danger of an injury to the defensive player. In fact, some football leagues do not allow cut blocks at all because of injury concern. Only use actual cut blocking in games and use stand-up dummies for drilling this block during practice.

Crack Block

A crack block is a block that is associated with a particular play, typically running plays to the outside—such as option plays, sweeps, and stretches. It is a fast-break block on an unsuspecting linebacker (or safety). Because of where he is aligned, the receiver can get a good angle on that inside defender. It is sometimes specifically tagged to a play (X crack or Z crack). The crack block is the wide receiver version of the blindside blitz, and it is fun because the player at whom it is directed has no clue that it is coming. Two ways to approach a crack block from the line of scrimmage are as follows:

- The receiver releases full speed directly toward his target.

- The receiver uses the push-crack method. Typically, he releases vertical for a couple of steps, pushes the defender back by selling deep, makes a head-and-shoulder fake to the outside, plants his outside foot, and breaks inside (like in a post break). He then runs at a full sprint toward his target—typically the linebacker or safety aligned inside.

Figure 8-10. Approaching the crack block on a linebacker or safety

In either scenario, the receiver cheats his splits in. His aiming point must be based on where the defender is going on the play, and not just his initial alignment. If the correct cutoff angle is not taken, the receiver will end up trailing the defender.

The receiver hits the defender at full speed with no breakdown or pauses. The key coaching point is that the receiver must hit the defender with his head in front of the defender's body. That is, the receiver gets his helmet in front of the defender's chest. Again, the receiver must be sure to keep his head and eyes up to reduce injury risk during this block. During the blow, one of the receiver's arms is in front, and the other arm is on the side of the defender.

Receivers need to be careful about penalties when using a crack block. If the receiver does not get his helmet across the front of the defender, he may receive a

Figure 8-11. Crack block on a linebacker or safety

penalty for blocking in the back. Teach receivers that if they can read the name of the pursued defender on the back of his jersey, the block will likely result in a penalty. The crack block must also be executed above the waist, or the receiver will be called for an illegal block below the waist. Although crack blocks must therefore be executed with extremely good technique, they are a great way for a receiver to light it up. More aggressive receivers will have fun executing them.

Stay Stuck Police

Staying on a block is a key to successful blocking, as is making a second effort. If the receiver misses his block or loses the defender, he must find someone else to block. Stay Stuck Police is one way to emphasize the importance of blocking. During practice, wear a bright red t-shirt with the words "Stay Stuck Police" printed on it. Using the blocking "crimes" form in Appendix E, record everyone (linemen, receivers, running backs, and even the quarterback) who misses a block, does not block through the whistle, or makes no second effort. For any blocking infringement, a player must stay after practice for punishment, which may be comprised of special conditioning work, 300 sit-ups, listening to selections read aloud from articles on the importance of blocking (with a quiz afterward), or listening to lectures from the coach on this topic. (Perhaps it is no surprise that players actually view listening to the lectures as more painful than the sit-ups.) Be careful not to use too much conditioning as punishment—especially before big games or late in the season when you do not want to go into key match-ups with tired legs.

The main objective of the Stay Stuck Police is to put emphasis on the importance of blocking and to make blocking a key theme for practices. After the first week it is introduced, bring out the shirt only randomly and expect big groans and lots of concern from the players about making the blocking crimes list. Just having players worrying about their name being on the list will significantly raise the blocking performance of the team.

Drills

Mirror and Stalk-Block Basics

Objective: To improve the receiver's ability to stalk block by focusing on mirroring, footwork, and hand moves

Equipment Needed: None

Setup: The receivers line up one yard apart and facing each other. One line is receivers, and the other is defenders.

Execution: Phase I—The mirror drill. The defender begins to shuffle back and forth in the direction the coach signals as though he were preparing to juke past the receiver to tackle a ballcarrier. The receiver mirrors the defender's moves while staying square with him. As the focus is on footwork in this phase of the drill, the receiver's hands should be behind his back.

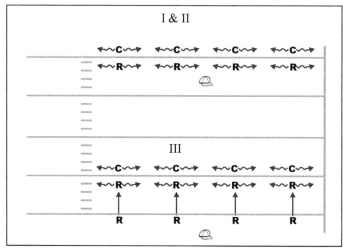

Figure 8-12. Mirror drill

Phase II—Hand moves. On the coach's command, the receivers add each of the following stalk-block hand techniques:

- Lock on and steer
- Punch and reload

Phase III—Move the receivers and defenders five yards away from each other. Again, the coach signals which way the defender should break. The receiver squares up the defender and executes the designated block until the whistle. Additionally, the punch-and-recoil move can be introduced at this depth.

Technique: Phase I—The receiver needs to keep his feet moving without crossing them and with a base slightly wider that his shoulders. He is in a low-coiled athletic position (head up, straight back, flexed knees).

Phase II—The receiver must attack with force from low to high and get his hands in the proper position. The punch and reload must be executed at a fast pace in conjunction with quickly moving feet.

Phase III—The receiver must stay square, maintain proper distance until the defender makes a move, shift his focus from the defender's belt buckle to his eyes upon contact, and lock his elbows during the block.

Common Errors:

- Receivers do not keep their feet moving fast enough.
- Receivers do not read the belt buckle of the defender.
- Receivers do not keep a wide enough base for balance, control, and speed.
- Receivers do not keep their eyes and head up as contact is initiated.
- Receivers play up too high.
- Receivers hold the defender.
- Receivers overextend and lunge.
- Receivers do not hold their blocks until the whistle.

Things to Yell:

- "Square up!"
- "Watch his belt buckle!"
- "Quick feet!"
- "Stay low!"
- "Low to high!" (the direction of the blow when the receiver makes contact with the defender)

Variation: Move the defender to a distance of 10 yards from the receiver. Have the receiver run full speed to and square up on the defender as he breaks down and before he begins mirroring and executing his block.

Stalk Block

Objective: To polish stalk-blocking skills in a game-like situation, and ensure that the receiver stays squared up on the defender and is aligned in between him and the ballcarrier

Equipment Needed: Two cones and one football

Setup: Cones are eight yards apart along a yard line. One receiver lines up by each cone. A defender lines up over each receiver in various leverages (inside, head-up, and outside) and at different depths throughout the drill. A running back aligns in the backfield area.

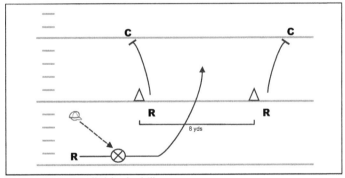

Figure 8-13. Stalk-block drill

Execution: At the snap, the coach pitches a ball to the running back, who takes a path upfield between the two receivers. The receivers release and stalk block until the coach's whistle.

Technique: Receivers use correct stalk-blocking technique:

- Mirroring
- Quick feet
- Low coiled body position
- Low-to-high thrust on contact
- Good hand and arm technique (lock on, punch-and-reload, punch-and-recoil)

Common Errors:

- The receiver does not move his feet quickly enough to stay squared up on the defender.
- The receiver does not thrust from low to high when he makes contact.
- The receiver overpursues and thus enables the defender to get past him to the ballcarrier.
- The receiver does not stay on the block long enough.

Things to Yell:

- "Break down!"
- "You overpursued!"
- "Square him up!"
- "Watch his belt buckle!"
- "Play lower!"
- "Low to high!"
- "Hold your block!"

Variation: Make a competition to see which receiver can hold his block longer.

Drive Block

Objective: To improve the receiver's ability to execute a drive block

Equipment Needed: One hand shield for each pair of receivers

Setup: Line one row of receivers along a yard line three yards apart. A row of defenders with hand shields are one yard away from and facing the receivers.

Execution: Phase I—At the coach's first whistle, the receiver starts his foot-fire. At the

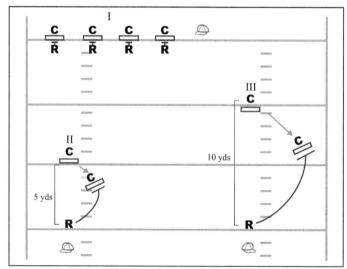

Figure 8-14. Drive-block drill

second whistle, he extends his arms and thrusts upward as he punches the defender's shield up over his head. The receiver stays locked onto the defender and keeps his feet moving until the coach's final whistle.

Phase II—Similar to Phase I, except:

- The defenders are now five yards away from the receivers before the initial contact.
- The coach varies the leverage of the defenders from head-up to inside to outside.
- The coach signals a direction for the defender to run (simulating running to attack the ballcarrier). The defender begins to take that angle. The receiver must take the correct angle to square up the defender, close the gap, and execute the drive block.

Phase III—The same as Phase II, except the defenders are now 10 yards away from the receivers. Now that the basic technique is installed, the distance here for the approach gives the receivers a more realistic feel for a game situation.

Technique: The receiver:

- Takes a correct angle on the defender
- Squares up the defender
- Closes the gap
- Uses his power center and thrusts from low to high for the blow
- Keeps his feet moving
- Stays locked on until the coach's whistle

Common Errors:

- The receiver does not take the correct angle and/or square up the defender.
- The receiver does not use the correct hand position.
- The receiver blocks the defender in the back.
- The receiver starts his block from a position that is too high and does not have enough thrust and upward momentum.
- The receiver does not aggressively attack the defender.
- The receiver does not keep his feet moving.
- The receiver does not stay on his block until the final whistle.

Things to Yell:

- "Square him up!"
- "Close the gap!"
- "Low to high!"
- "Keep your head and eyes up!"

- "Keep driving your feet!"
- "Stay on him!"

Push Crack

Objective: To improve the receiver's ability to execute an effective crack block with a push on the cornerback first

Equipment Needed: None

Setup: Align a cornerback five yards off of a receiver. Position another defender at the same depth and five yards inside the cornerback. He is playing a linebacker.

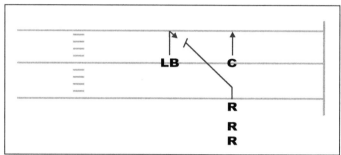

Figure 8-15. Push-crack drill

Execution: At the snap, the defenders backpedal five yards. The receiver releases hard off the line, pushes a couple of yards upfield at the cornerback, and cuts sharply inside to execute a crack block on the linebacker. The coach assigns the flow of the linebacker (continues to backpedal, moves forward, or moves across the field).

Technique:

- The receiver bursts off the line, sells deep, and plants on his outside foot with a quick head fake to get the cornerback's hips turned.
- The receiver cuts across the field at an angle that enables him to lay a proper crack block on the linebacker. The receiver keeps his helmet in front of the linebacker and hits him above the waist.

Common Errors:

- Receivers do not run straight at the cornerback to push him off and start to move inside too soon.
- Receivers take the wrong angle and end up chasing the linebacker from the rear or hitting him on the backside, which leads to a penalty.
- Receivers block with their heads down instead of looking at their target.

Things to Yell:

- "Sell deep!"
- "Get flatter!"
- "Anticipate where he is going!"

- "Get your head in front!"
- "Keep your head and eyes up!"

Cut Block

Objective: To improve the receiver's cut-blocking technique without risk of injury to receivers or defensive players

Equipment Needed: One stand-up dummy

Setup: A receiver holding a stand-up dummy is 10 yards away from the line of receivers and with inside or outside leverage.

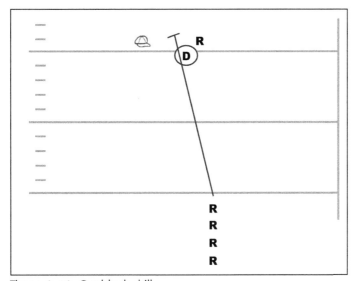

Figure 8-16. Cut-block drill

Execution: At the whistle, the receiver releases, runs to, and cuts the dummy.

Technique: The receiver bursts off the line toward the dummy, throws his right shoulder to the opposite (i.e., right) side of the dummy, rolls into the dummy, and keeps rolling with his knees flexed. He continues until the play is whistled dead by the coach.

Common Errors:

- The receiver dives too low on the dummy. Remember: the aiming point is the defender's thigh area.
- The receiver quits rolling before the whistle.

Things to Yell:

- "Throw higher!"
- "Keep rolling!"
- "Attack the dummy!"

Variation: Have the receivers run to the dummy, break down, shoot their hands to the dummy (stalk block), and execute the cut block from this stalk-block position.

Second Effort

Objective: To work on speed and intensity in blocking as well as on releases and playing through the whistle

Equipment Needed: One football

Setup: A receiver lines up with a cornerback jamming him at the line. A safety is 12 yards downfield and 8 yards inside.

Execution: At the snap, the receiver breaks the jam of the cornerback and runs to stalk block a safety until the coach's first whistle. Then the receiver drops down and bear-crawls until the coach's final whistle. The bear crawl indirectly simulates the second effort needed to find someone else to block when the ballcarrier suddenly breaks free.

Technique: The receiver gets an inside release, stays on the stalk block with the defender, bear-crawls quickly, and continues through the final whistle.

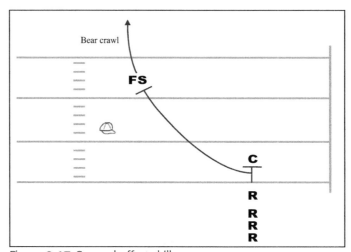

Figure 8-17. Second-effort drill

Common Errors:

- Receivers lose their intensity during the drill.
- Receivers release too slowly at the line (engage too long with the cornerback).
- Receivers let the safety escape the block before the whistle.
- Receivers stop the bear crawl before the whistle.

Things to Yell:

- "Rip through him!"
- "Go! Go! Go!"
- "Square him up!"
- "Watch his belt buckle!"
- "Play low!"
- "Hold your block!"

- "Don't quit!"
- "Great job!"

Variation: If a disciplinary point needs to be made, run the drill horizontally beginning at one sideline and have the players bear-crawl completely across the field. Doing so can give you a lot of insight into your players' characters (especially after several consecutive reps of this drill).

Sled Drills

Sled work helps receivers work on the low-to-high thrust and lock-on needed to effectively stalk block or drive block and includes the correct hand position (thumbs up). This work is done on the sled from two positions:

- The receivers start on their knees and sit back on their heels. They thrust up and forward and punch and reload the sled. If you don't have a sled available, this drill can be executed with a defender holding a dummy.

- The receivers start from a two-point stance (squared up on the sled) with knees flexed and body coiled. They thrust from low to high as they lock on and drive the sled across the field.

YARDS AFTER THE CATCH

Chapter Nine

The yards-after-the-catch (YAC), a.k.a. run-after-the-catch (RAC), is a very important part of the receiver's job. This chapter analyzes the key components of yards-after-the-catch in the order that they occur—secure the football, accelerate after the catch, gain yards, and protect the football. Drills are provided to help ingrain this aspect of the game in your receivers' minds and in their muscle memory. Your receivers will improve in this area when you give time and attention to it in practice.

Secure the Football

Obviously, you can have no "YA" without "C." After the receiver catches the football, he tucks the ball away while looking it all the way in (Chapter 2). The football should be secured in the tuck position before the receiver initiates other aspects of YAC.

Accelerate After the Catch

One part of a receiver's YAC technique that should be included in every moving practice rep is turning quickly upfield and accelerating after the catch. Just as it is imperative to accelerate through the break, the receiver must accelerate after the catch to gain further separation from the defender. During practice, receivers often catch the ball and just jog back to get lined up for the next rep. Accelerating after the catch needs to be enforced every day on every catch. Accelerating after the catch with the ball tightly tucked and gaining yards (five-yard minimum in drills) should be schooled until it is automatic. When a catch occurs in a game, the receiver should not ever have to think about any of these mechanics.

Gain Yards

The receiver must determine the best way to gain as many yards as possible by running north and south, and executing escape moves before being tackled. The factors that a receiver uses to determine where and how to get upfield include:

- The route he is running.
- The location of the defender(s).
- The position and the momentum of the ball as he catches it.

General rules include:

- If the receiver is already running upfield while making the catch, such as on a post or fade, he should simply use his upfield momentum to keep running— putting his jets on to the max.
- If the receiver is running crossfield while making the catch (such as on a dig or cross), he should look for the quickest way to turn his crossfield path upfield to gain positive yardage.
- On routes where the receiver is coming back to the football (e.g., stop and curl), the rule of thumb is that to get upfield the receiver should first make as tight a

turn as possible outside and away from defenders coming from the middle of the field. Once a receiver has become skilled at catching and turning outside, he may add a quick head fake to the inside to misdirect the closest defender before pivoting outside. However, if the ball's position causes the receiver to turn inside for the catch, he needs to use that momentum to continue his upfield progression, instead of changing direction to turn the long way around to the outside. (It is interesting to note that because offenses trained their receivers to routinely turn outside after the catch on stops and curls, defenders were consistently attacking the receiver's outside shoulder. Some programs therefore now tell their receivers to turn inside after the catch on these routes. This approach has improved their YAC statistics on these routes. The defenders fly by the outside shoulder of the receiver as he pivots inside and runs upfield.)

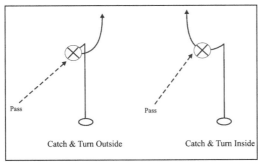

Figure 9-1. Catch and get upfield by spinning inside or outside

Run North-South

On all types of routes, the receiver needs to be sure to run north and south as soon as possible after the catch, as opposed to moving laterally too far across the field. Some receivers take too much time looking for the perfect hole between or around the defenders instead of turning upfield quickly and taking whatever yards they can get.

Split the Defenders

When two defenders are approaching a receiver, he should split the defenders ("catch and knife") and get as many yards as possible instead of running crossfield to try to get around them. The receiver must:

- Find the path between the two defenders that gives each of them the least likelihood of making the tackle.

- Gain the most yards possible by keeping his legs moving as he gets hit and as the tacklers wrap him up.

Escape Moves

Besides running north-south, receivers can use several techniques to escape defenders. Of course, the best situation is if you have very talented receivers who naturally have the moves and don't need to be taught how to escape defenders. If not, several techniques can be taught to receivers to help them elude defenders including the plain juke, the stutter step, and the spin move.

Plain Juke

In the plain juke, the receiver makes a head-and-shoulder fake in one direction to mislead the defender and runs the opposite direction of the fake. This move needs to be as fluid a part of the running motion as possible.

Stutter Step

The stutter step is best used as the defender approaches the receiver head-on, and is breaking down to make a tackle. The receiver quickly chops his feet in place, makes a head-and-shoulder fake, and runs the opposite way past the defender. The chopping feet help to freeze the defender, and the head-and-shoulder fake should seduce the defender into turning the wrong direction. The keys are for the receiver to have super-quick feet and to focus his eyes in the direction he does *not* want to go.

Spin Move

The spin move is a last resort, and is used when a defender has moved in to tackle. Upon contact, the receiver spins around and away from the defender. Emphasis should be on protecting the football during this move because spinning may leave the ball vulnerable to a strip as the receiver's arms are utilized in propelling the spin move.

Protect the Football

When the receiver is in heavy traffic or is about to be tackled, he needs to secure the football with both hands to prevent fumbles. The preferred method is for the receiver to use running-back technique and squeeze the ball with both arms into his stomach area immediately before contact. Alternatively, he can simply take his off hand and place it over the top of the football. Here, his hand comes clear across his body and double-secures the ball in the outside arm.

Whichever method is used, the receiver needs to bend his shoulders forward and use his upper body to envelop the football. It is imperative to protect the football with every means possible.

Figure 9-2. Protect the football

Defenders are currently taught more and more to go for a strip, and not just to make the tackle. After the ballcarrier is secured with one arm, the defender uses his other hand to strip the ball. Alternatively, one defender may initiate a tackle and hold up a receiver as the second defender goes in for the strip. The key to preventing the strip is for the receiver to squeeze the ball in traffic with significant pressure—especially from the elbow.

While a receiver who is about to be tackled generally needs to protect the football, at times he must stretch out and extend the ball for extra yardage. The receiver must be aware of all conditions in the game to judge when it is appropriate to expose the football in this way. He must consider questions such as:

- How desperate is the team for the touchdown or for the first down that can be gained only by extending the football forward in his hand?

- What's the risk/return ratio for extra yardage versus a turnover given where the team is on the field, the score, and the time left in the game?

- How important is maintaining possession of the football to run down the clock?

Drills

Split the Defenders

Objective: To improve a receiver's ability to both protect the football and gain the most yards possible as he runs between two defenders who are approaching at different angles.

Equipment Needed: Two footballs, two hand shields, and two cones

Setup: Receivers line up perpendicular to a yard line. The coach is 10 yards away from them at an angle toward the middle of the field. Two defenders with hand shields line up eight yards apart and five yards upfield from the receiver. The goal line is marked with two cones that are 10 yards from the starting point.

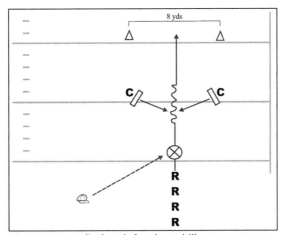

Figure 9-3. Split-the-defenders drill

Execution: The coach throws a quick pass to the receiver, who runs upfield. He makes any needed adjustments in his path so he can successfully run to the goal line between the oncoming defenders. The defenders make contact but do not tackle or take down the receiver.

Technique: After successfully catching and tucking the football, the receiver accelerates upfield between the two defenders and past the cones. As the defenders close in on him, the receiver secures the football with both hands, lowers his shoulders, prepares for contact and/or to be stripped, and keeps his legs moving.

Common Errors:

- The receiver does not accelerate full speed after the catch.
- The receiver runs east-west to try to go around the oncoming defenders instead of running straight upfield between them and taking whatever yards he can get.
- The receiver does not protect the football.

Things to Yell:

- "Accelerate upfield!"
- "Run north-south!"
- "Squeeze the ball!"
- "Keep your legs moving!"

Variations:

- The defenders may be aligned in various positions so that their angles of attack change and the receiver must adjust accordingly.
- This may be done as a full-blown tackling and takedown drill with one defender tackling and one going for the strip.

Juke

Objective: To develop a receiver's ability to juke a defender and get by him in the open field

Equipment Needed: Two footballs, two cones, and four hand shields

Setup: Four defenders with hand shields line up two rows deep, five yards apart, and face each other in gauntlet-type formation. A fifth defender, without a hand shield, is stationed five yards behind the second row of defenders. Two cones are placed 10 yards behind him, and five yards apart. The receivers are lined up opposite the fifth defender and five yards perpendicular to the path they will take through the gauntlet. The coach is five yards back and five yards to the side of the receivers.

Execution: On the coach's command, the first receiver jogs in front of him. The coach throws him a pass, which the receiver catches and secures. Then he turns upfield through the two lines of defenders with hand shields. As he does so, the defenders bat at the receiver and the ball. After he clears the second line of defenders, the receiver faces the lone remaining defender. His goal is to juke that defender in such a way that he scores by running through the two cones.

Technique: The receiver accelerates upfield after the catch, protects the football as he runs through the gauntlet, and then jukes the defender while bursting through the cones.

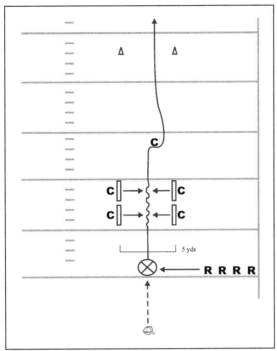

Figure 9-4. Juke drill

Common Errors:

- The receiver turns upfield too quickly before he has secured the catch.
- The receiver does not turn tightly upfield.
- The receiver does not accelerate upfield after the catch.
- The receiver runs too high through the gauntlet, does not protect the football, and does not have forward body lean.
- The receiver fumbles the football.
- The receiver is unable to effectively juke the last defender.
- The receiver does not accelerate through the cones.

Things to Yell:

- "Accelerate at the catch!"
- "Run north-south!"
- "Forward body lean!"
- "Keep your feet moving!"
- "Protect the football!"
- "Squeeze your elbow!"
- "Make a move!"

Variation: Instead of the fifth defender simply making the receiver juke, he may actually move in on the receiver to tackle him and/or strip the football.

Sideline YAC

Objective: To teach a receiver to turn upfield quickly in a very narrow space without going out of bounds

Equipment Needed: Two footballs

Setup: Receivers line up horizontally across the football field approximately 10 yards from the sideline. The coach stands in front of the first receiver and approximately five yards away.

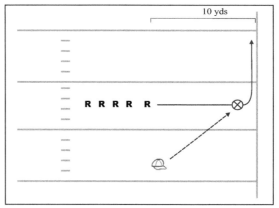

Figure 9-5. Sideline YAC drill

Execution: The receiver runs full speed toward the sideline (simulating an out route) and catches the ball approximately one or two yards before the sideline. The receiver tucks the ball in his outside arm and turns upfield while staying inbounds.

Technique: The receiver catches the ball, turns, and accelerates upfield without going out of bounds. The turn must be quick and tight.

Common Errors:

- The receiver does not catch the football because he turns upfield too early.
- The receiver does not tuck the ball in his outside arm.
- The receiver does not make his turn tight enough to stay inbounds.
- The receiver does not accelerate after the catch.

Things to Yell:

- "Make the catch first!"
- "Tight turn!"
- "Accelerate!"
- "Get upfield!"

BRING ON THE DEFENSE

Chapter Ten

This chapter discusses which individual routes and route packages are most effective against man and zone coverages. It introduces rotating and combination coverages, and explains hot routes and scrambling. In the figures that follow, the circled defenders are the defenders whom the quarterback is reading in his pass progression.

Effective Individual Routes Versus Man Coverage

Types of routes that generally work well against man coverage include:

- Routes where the receiver keeps moving (drag, cross, speed-out) with his defender trailing him.

- Routes where the receiver gains separation from the defender with a plant in his route stem (stop, curl, comeback, slant).

- Downfield routes when the receiver runs away from the free safety (go, fade, corner). Fade and go routes are especially effective because it's easy for the receiver to catch the ball without the defender knowing where the ball is until the last second, since the defender is only looking at the receiver.

- Post routes if a free safety is not in the middle of the field.

- Double-move (combination) routes (e.g., hitch-and-go, slant-fade, post-dig, and post-corner) when the defender bites on the fake.

- Pick routes. Theoretically illegal, these routes are highly effective. Just don't make it too obvious or you'll get a flag. (See Chapter 3.)

In pure man, once the receiver has his man beat, he scores if he catches the ball.

Effective Route Packages Versus Man Coverage

Packages that work well against man coverage utilize the previously mentioned routes. Many different combinations of these routes can be successfully used to create packages to defeat man coverage. These packages are not listed here because the permutations are so many, and because the real key to success versus man coverage is simply the personnel match-up. That is, the ability of your receiver to defeat his defender in hand-to-hand combat—whether it be releasing at the line, getting open on the stem of the route, losing the defender at the breakpoint or catching the pass with the defender draped all over him.

Effective Individual Routes Versus Cover 2

- Corner: A corner route reaches a window in the coverage over the cornerback who sits in the flat and under the safety who is protecting the deep half.

- Out: An out route hits the window in the coverage over the cornerback and under the safety.

- Fade: The fade has splashdown in the window over the cornerback and under the safety.

- Curl: The safeties are backpedaling so they do not get beat deep, and it is difficult for the linebackers to see and get an angle on the receiver running a curl behind them.

- Dig: The middle of the field is usually open in cover two since the two safeties are dropping toward the deep halves.

- Post: The middle of the field is vulnerable. This pass should be thrown under the backpedaling safeties.

Effective Route Packages Versus Cover 2

Play One: Stops, Corners

The stop routes occupy the cornerback. The corner routes are run on an angle away from the near safety and at a shorter depth than the safety's drop will take him.

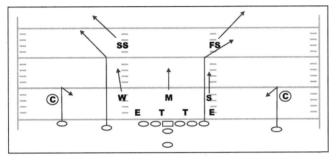

Figure 10-1. Cover 2 weaknesses: play one

Play Two: Verticals, Post (or Dig)

The cornerbacks are in trail technique on the verticals. The safeties' initial drops take them toward the deep sidelines to protect against the outside threats from the verticals. The go-to route (post) breaks underneath the level of the safeties in the middle of the field. Alternatively, use a dig route here instead of a post. The tight end may also be open if the free safety goes with the outside vertical.

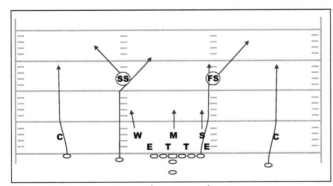

Figure 10-2. Cover 2 weaknesses: play two

Play Three: Fades, Speed-Outs

The speed-outs hold the cornerbacks. The safeties have a lot of grass to cover to catch the receivers on fade routes. In fact, if the ball is correctly thrown, the safeties should not be able to make a play on it. If the cornerbacks go with the receivers on their fade routes, the speed-outs will be wide open.

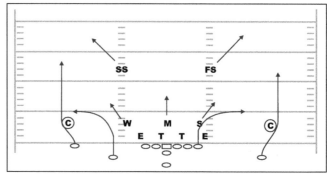

Figure 10-3. Cover 2 weaknesses: play three

Play Four: Curl, Wheel, Flat, Post

The cornerback may squat on the speed-out part of the wheel route (especially if he has been set up by previous play calling to do so) or the flat route. If he does follow the inside receiver deep, he will generally be in a trail position on the wheel route. Thus, the slot receiver will be open in the window above the cornerback and below the dropping near safety. The curl may also be open. The curl receiver reads the linebacker's drop and finds the open window. He cuts at the breakpoint and either comes back to the ball at a 45-degree angle or slides horizontally toward the middle of the field to find that open window.

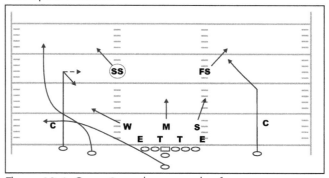

Figure 10-4. Cover 2 weaknesses: play four

Play Five: Fade, Out, Speed-Out (flood package)

The cornerback sits in the flat to cover the speed-out. The safety must pick one of the two deep receivers to cover, which leaves one of the receivers open. If the cornerback drops with one of the deeper receivers, the speed-out will be open.

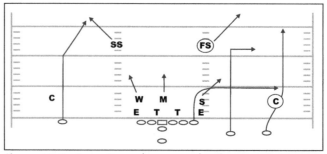

Figure 10-5. Cover 2 weaknesses: play five

Play Six: Out, Corner, Cross, Post

The cornerback either jumps the out route, which leaves the cross open, or plays strict zone and waits for the cross route to penetrate his zone, which opens up the square-out. In either case, the corner route occupies the safety.

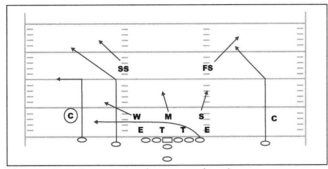

Figure 10-6. Cover 2 weaknesses: play six

Effective Individual Routes Versus Cover 3

- Speed-outs: Linebackers and strong safeties have a significant amount of turf to cover to get to the flats, and are not typically the fastest guys on the field. Therefore, passes to speedy receivers in the flats make for favorable match-ups.

- Stop: With cornerbacks backpedaling to the deep thirds, this ball is caught by outside receivers underneath the defense for a "sure" five-yard gain.

- Curl: The linebackers have to cover a big area (hook and curl zones).

- Comeback: This route hits near the sideline between the zones of the deep cornerback and the flat player.

- Dig/square-in: This route works because the receiver gets open in a window behind the linebackers and in front of the safety in the middle of the field.

- Square-out: This route is run to the window underneath the cornerback's zone and above the flat defender.

Effective Route Packages Versus Cover 3

Play One: Fade, Out, Flat, Post

The fade occupies the cornerback and the linebacker/strong safety must pick between the two routes in his zone—the out route by the slot receiver and the flat route of the running back.

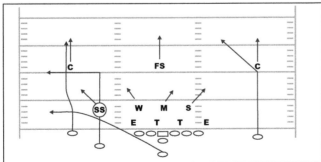

Figure 10-7. Cover 3 weaknesses: play one

Play Two: Curl, Wheel, Flat, Post

The curl route gets open in a window behind the linebackers/strong safety. The wheel route occupies the cornerback. The flat route occupies the strong safety underneath. Alternatively, the flat route is open in front of the strong safety if he covers the curl.

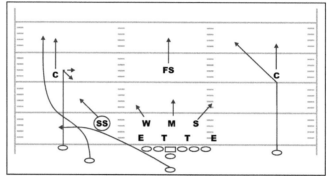

Figure 10-8. Cover 3 weaknesses: play two

Play Three: Slants, Speed-Outs

The safety or linebacker (depending on which side the play is run) must choose to cover either the slant or the speed-out—both are in his zone.

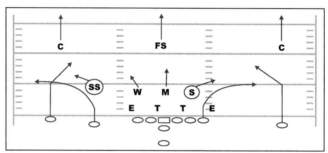

Figure 10-9. Cover 3 weaknesses: play three

Play Four: Dig, Wheel, Post

The twinside cornerback goes deep with the wheel. The free safety must cover the post because it is the deepest threat. Thus the dig gets open, as it is hard for a dropping linebacker/strong safety to get the right angle on and make a play on the dig route.

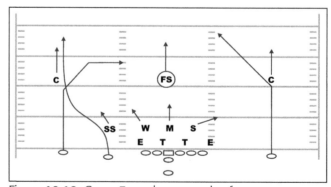

Figure 10-10. Cover 3 weaknesses: play four

Play Five: Fade, Out, Speed-Out (flood package), Post

This package sends three offensive players into two defensive zones—the cornerback's zone and the strong safety's zone. The cornerback takes the fade and leaves the strong safety to cover both the out and the speed-out.

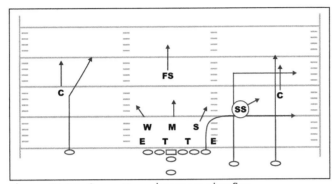

Figure 10-11. Cover 3 weaknesses: play five

Play Six: Four Verticals With a Comeback Option

Receivers must stay on their landmarks: the numbers for outside receivers and usually the hash marks for inside receivers. Doing so ensures enough separation so that one defender cannot cover two receivers. The free safety in the middle of the field has to pick which inside vertical route to cover. If the cornerbacks are playing with very soft coverage, an additional option is that the outside receivers can convert their vertical routes to comebacks for a completion near the sideline.

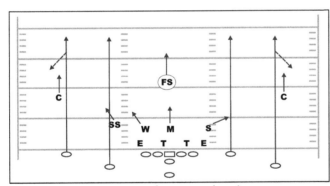

Figure 10-12. Cover 3 weaknesses: play six

Effective Individual Routes Versus Cover 4

- Stop: With cornerbacks backpedaling to the deep quarters, this ball is caught by outside receivers underneath the defense for a "sure" five-yard gain.

- Speed-out: The corners backpedal on the snap and the linebackers trail the receiver into the flats.

- Square-out: This route is run underneath the cornerback's zone and on top of the linebacker's zone.

- Post: The deep middle of the field is vulnerable because the safeties normally initially do not drop since they are playing the run first (unless it is a prevent cover four).

Effective Route Packages Versus Cover 4

Play One: Fade, Speed-Out (or Slant), Post

The fade occupies the cornerback, and the linebacker trails the receiver on his speed-out. If the linebacker aligns outside and anticipates a speed-out, a common adjustment is for the inside receiver to convert his route to a slant.

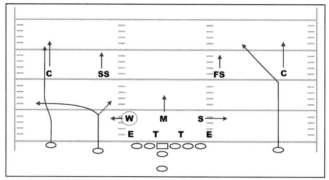

Figure 10-13. Cover 4 weaknesses: play one

Play Two: Fade, Out, Post

The fade occupies the cornerback and the linebacker cannot catch up with the receiver on his out route. If the cornerback does bite on the out, the fade will be open.

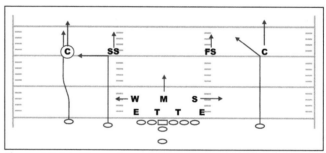

Figure 10-14. Cover 4 weaknesses: play two

Play Three: Slants (or Stops)

The cornerbacks backpedal at the snap, which leaves the outside slants or stops open. The two inside receivers occupy the sitting safeties. The defense will probably make a tackle on the play, but not until the ball is caught for a gain.

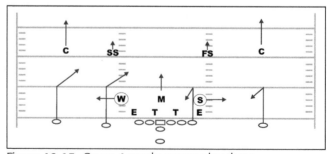

Figure 10-15. Cover 4 weaknesses: play three

Play Four: Comebacks, Speed-Outs

The straight stem of the comeback route pushes the cornerback deep, and the break toward the sideline enables the receiver to gain separation. This approach works well when the cornerback has been sensitized (or hopefully burned) by several reps of the fade first. The inside receiver on the speed-out route is another option since the linebacker trails this receiver to the flats.

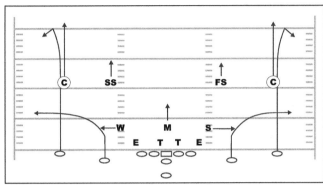

Figure 10-16. Cover 4 weaknesses: play four

Play Five: Stops (or Speed-Outs), Corners

The corner routes occupy the cornerbacks, and the linebackers have trouble covering the shorter routes in the flat.

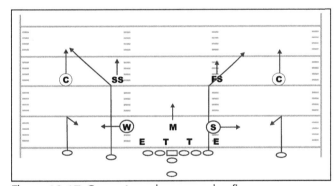

Figure 10-17. Cover 4 weaknesses: play five

Play Six: Dig, Wheel, Curl, Post

The cornerback on the left covers the wheel route. The safeties are occupied by the dig

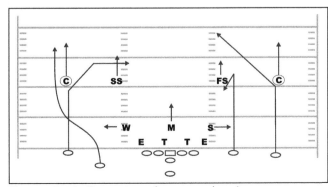

Figure 10-18. Cover 4 weaknesses: play six

and the curl routes. The post gets open behind the safeties because the cornerback on the right stays in his quarter of the field.

Rotating Coverages

Defenses sometimes rotate coverages, which means they line up in one coverage and move to another. Rotating coverages have several aspects:

Disguise

Offenses have become more sophisticated—and so have defenses. Quarterbacks and receivers are taught to make pre-snap reads that tell them what to audible to and, in the case of receivers, how to amend their routes for maximum success versus a particular defense. To counteract this tactic, defenses have become very skilled at disguising coverages by showing one coverage and shifting to another.

Pre-Snap Rotations

Defenses can adjust to certain formations or personnel packages that the offense lines up in. For example, a defense bases in cover 2 but elects to play cover 3 versus trips. Therefore, every time an offense comes out in a trips formation, the defense adjusts and rolls to cover 3 instead of staying in their cover-2 base. The defense must also make the same adjustment if the offense motions from another formation to trips.

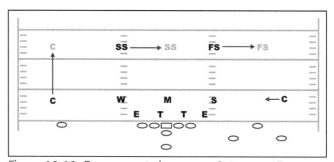

Figure 10-19. Pre-snap rotation: cover 2 to cover 3

Defenses may adjust to create favorable personnel match-ups by putting the best defender on the best receiver. Also, defenses may rotate to stymie particular plays the offense has used successfully. For example, if the offense normally runs a stretch play to the alley from a particular formation, the best way to defend it may be by switching responsibilities between the cover-2 cornerback and safety on that side. In this situation, the safety, who is already lined up in the alley, walks up to be in a better

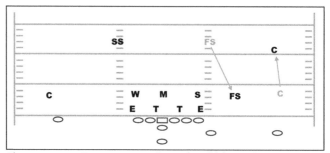

Figure 10-20. Pre-snap rotation: cloud/sky or invert

position to stop the run. The cornerback bails to cover the deep half of the field. Some defenses call this coverage "cloud/sky" to indicate whether primary run support is handled by the cornerback (cloud) or the safety (sky). Others call invert (switch) to signal players to trade responsibilities.

Post-Snap Rotations

Defenses can also adjust based on what the offense does after the snap. One example is cover-2 read. In this coverage, the safety and cornerback to one side of the ball read the receivers' routes to determine which defender should cover each receiver. For example, if the inside receiver runs a route to the flat, the cornerback covers him, and the free safety is responsible for the fade. If the inside receiver runs a skinny post, the free safety covers him, and the cornerback runs deep with the outside receiver.

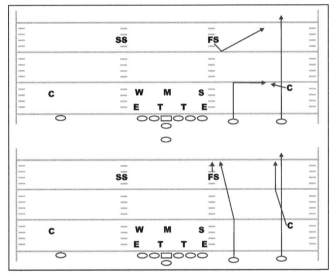

Figure 10-21. Post-snap rotation: cover-2 read

Also, some defenses roll the secondary to one side or the other depending on the flow of the play. For example, the defense aligns in cover 2 but plans to roll to cover 3 at the snap. To decide which way to roll, the defense keys which direction the quarterback opens to. If he opens to his left, the cornerback to that side sits and becomes the cover-3 strong safety, the safety to that side becomes the right-deep-third defender, the other safety becomes the middle-third defender, and the backside cornerback covers the far-deep third of the field.

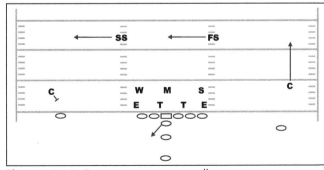

Figure 10-22. Post-snap coverage roll

Combination Coverages

Zone/Zone

Zone coverages may be combined together so that one type of zone coverage is used on one half of the field, and a different coverage is used on the other half. One of these combo coverages is quarter-quarter-halves in which the defense plays cover 2 on one half of the field and plays quarters coverage on the other half. When the football is on a hash mark, quarter-quarter-halves is often used to gain more pass support on the wideside of the field by having two deep zone players there instead of just one.

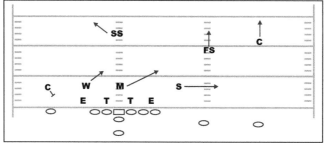

Figure 10-23. Combination coverages—cover 2/4

Zone/Man

Zone coverages may also be combined with man coverage to produce defenses like two-deep-man-under. This coverage is used when you want the aggressiveness of man-to-man play up front but the insurance of having two deep safety players. Alternatively, defenses may run man coverage on one side of the field and zone coverage on the other. This approach is generally used to get an extra player in zone coverage on the wideside of the field while leaving the star cornerback to cover a receiver man-to-man on the shortside of the field.

Hot Routes

Hot routes are used to take advantage of sudden holes in the defense. Hot routes are used in two types of situations. The first situation is when a receiver is uncovered (no one aligns over him). The receiver and the quarterback use a subtle signal to indicate that they have both recognized the situation. The quarterback immediately initiates the snap and throws quickly to this uncovered receiver who runs a pre-designated route.

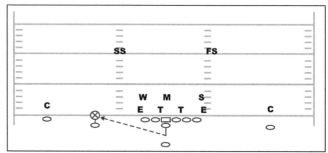

Figure 10-24. Hot (uncovered) receiver

The other use of hot routes is with automatic checks the offense uses when it reads blitz. These routes are designed to be run (typically by a tight end, wing, or slot receiver) into the void created by a blitzing linebacker or strong safety. This situation is also true for an outside receiver who becomes hot when a cornerback blitzes. The key to success is that both the quarterback and the designated receiver read blitz and are able to quickly and automatically execute their hot assignments.

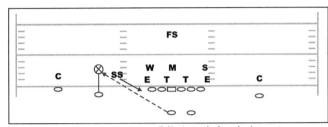

Figure 10-25. Hot receiver (blitzing defender)

Scrambling

Scrambling occurs when the quarterback is chased out of the pocket by penetrating defenders. When receivers recognize that the called play has broken down, they need to automatically go into scrambling mode. While specific rules vary from program to program, general concepts are as follows.

Each receiver immediately breaks off his route and runs his designated scramble path. If the receiver is running a route to the middle of the field or to the side opposite from where the quarterback is scrambling, he must come off his route and work flat across the field back in the direction of the scramble. If the receiver is running a shorter route on the same side of the field as the scramble, he needs to work to and/or up the sideline and look for a deep ball. If the receiver is running a deeper route on the same side of the field as the scramble, he needs to turn and work at a slight angle back downfield and toward that sideline. With all flow thus coming to his side of the field, the quarterback has multiple options and an easier pass because he does not have to throw across his body to the backside of the field. Because of the chaotic nature of the situation, receivers need to keep their eyes on the quarterback and keep moving until they get—and stay—open. After the quarterback throws the ball or if he runs, the receivers must identify the key defensive threats to make the most effective blocks possible. Numerous scrambling scenarios are possible. Three common scenarios are shown in Figure 10-26.

Drills

Scramble

Objective: To improve the receivers' ability to react to a quarterback scramble

Equipment Needed: Two footballs

Setup: The receivers line up in an offensive formation (preferably a four-receiver set).

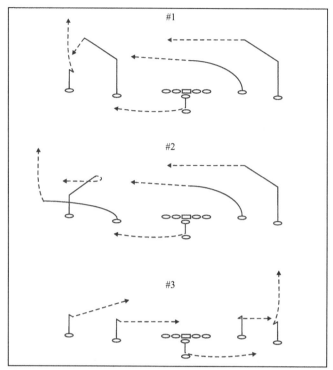

Figure 10-26. Selected scramble scenarios

Execution: The coach calls an offensive play. The offense starts to run the play. On the whistle, the quarterback scrambles, and the receivers adjust their routes.

Technique: As soon as the quarterback starts to scramble, the receivers adjust their routes according to their program's scramble rules. The quarterback throws or runs. If the quarterback runs, or if the ball goes to another receiver, the remaining receivers must quickly adjust to make effective blocks.

Common Errors:

- Receivers do not take the correct paths after breaking off their routes.
- Receivers do not maintain enough separation between each other.
- Receivers do not keep moving until the play is over.

Things to Yell:

- "Scramble!"
- "Adjust your route!"
- "Keep moving!"
- "Come back to the ball!"
- "Find someone to block!"

PSYCHOLOGY

Football coaching is psychological. It involves motivating, disciplining, teaching, and caring. This is especially true in coaching wide receivers. If you are lucky, you will have very talented athletes who thus far have relied on their natural talents—speed, agility, hands—but who, because they are gifted, may be undisciplined and not have much of a work ethic. Often, you will have less talented athletes who may need help in areas such as persistence and self-confidence. Usually though, you will have a wide range of personalities to deal with and win over.

Passion

Regardless of the talent of your receivers and your level of football, one of the most important traits you can show is passion: passion for your players and passion for the game that they are playing and that you are coaching. Passion consists of excitement, devotion, love, involvement, attention, and—very important—energy transfer. If you truly have passion for the game of football, your receivers will see that in you, and your energy and enthusiasm will be contagious. If you don't have passion for football, you're in the wrong profession. If your enthusiasm for your job is waning a bit, think about the fact that hundreds of guys are driving home tonight past football fields and dreaming of being you.

Show the Love

Another key ingredient is showing the love. Everybody craves this today. Kids in high school and middle school need to feel the love from other adults besides their parents. Even college kids crave it. Let's face it—adults do, too. "Show the love" whenever you can. This encompasses everything from making things fun, to setting high standards, to being consistent with the individual and across the group. However, the most significant thing a coach can do is to show his athletes that he believes in them, even when they don't believe in themselves. No matter how difficult or moody the athlete, and no matter how ridiculous the stunt he has just performed on the field (or off the field), if you look in a player's eyes and say, "I believe in you even when you don't believe in yourself," it is hard for a young person to turn away from that.

Anger: Use It Wisely

While your coaching style is dictated by your personality, it is important to consider when the use of "ripping" athletes for mistakes is useful, and when it is not. Occasionally coaches may allow their anger or frustration to get the better of them, and they sometimes lose their tempers indiscriminately. Anger is a much more valuable tool when you use it as a specific means to an end (e.g., for a certain type of motivation or when a particular player needs to be brought up short for a specific reason). If you use anger and yelling less often, you will find it has much more impact when you do use it. (You may also find that it preserves your vocal cords for a longer period of time through the season.)

Positive Reinforcement

The issue of negative versus positive reinforcement is interesting in football and in life. Of course, the use of positive or negative reinforcement is something that must reflect your personality, your program's philosophy, and the personality and character of your players. Generally, though, it is preferable to reward good performances with positive things as opposed to punishing bad performances with up-downs, gassers, fingertip push-ups, and so forth. Although some of these techniques may be needed to get players' attention, to set a tone in practice, or to reeducate a recalcitrant receiver, they should be used selectively.

Sometimes with some groups, it may initially seem like the punishment type of system works more effectively than the reward type. In those cases, try to switch their motivational hot buttons from negative to positive.

Learn From It and Move On

When you read other football books, an expression commonly applied to the cornerback position is that you need athletes with short memories—athletes who can learn quickly from a mistake, shake off a bad play, and move on to the next play. Stewing or grinding on a mistake or asking "What if…?" is a waste of energy. Learning to let it go and move forward quickly is a very valuable life skill that all the players on the football field should learn—and receivers especially so. Receivers are often in the spotlight, where everyone in the stadium is watching them either catch the touchdown pass or drop it in the end zone. It takes a lot of guts to come back from a big mistake and play harder, better, and faster on the next play, but that is what football and life require. Learning from a mistake and quickly moving on is a tool your receivers will use long after their gridiron days are over.

Do Unto Others

Kids think they are adults, and they all want to be treated like adults. One way to coach kids is, therefore, to actually treat them like adults until they prove they cannot be treated that way. While it may sound shocking, this technique is surprisingly effective. You might treat your players somewhat like clients, which does not mean clients in the sense that they have a choice of what to do or whether to work hard on a drill. However, sometimes when you present things, you might give the receiver an option of how he feels more comfortable doing something. Ask his opinion (he must be able to explain why he prefers a certain way) and you might learn something valuable in the answer. When you talk about non-football things, you might say, "Here are what I see as your options, but it's obviously up to you to make the call," instead of just always issuing a decree. This line is difficult to balance because you must keep the discipline and respect of your players, but at the same time you don't need to be autocratic while you are doing that. Fundamentally, it comes down to "what goes around comes around." When you treat your kids with respect and decency (really a form of showing the love), over time, they will usually respond in kind (yes, even wild, unruly ones), and sometimes when it matters most: when the game—literally or figuratively—is on the line.

Maximum Effort

Human nature causes people to sometimes try to get away with the least possible effort that doesn't lead to failure—and that observation is especially true of teenagers. Sometimes receivers do not try hard or do not run full speed on every rep. However, the intricacies of football and the interdependence of the 11 men on the field require that maximum effort must be given by the individual on every practice rep, or everyone's time is wasted (10 other offensive players, coaches, scout team, etc.).

My high school principal used to say, "The true measure of a man's worth is what he would do if he knew he would never be found out." In other words, a receiver should always burst off the line, engage the defender energetically, and hold his block through the whistle—even when he thinks the run play is going to the other side of the field and no one is watching him.

Work Hard

Hard work is obviously necessary for a corps of receivers on a football team to be successful. As Benjamin Franklin said, "Diligence is the mother of good luck." The concept of work hard has several components:

- Perseverance
- Determination
- Grit
- Overcoming obstacles
- Goal setting and working until those goals are met
- Lots of effective reps so muscle memory and mental memory of a technique or play become automatic (if a player has to think as a play unfolds, he'll be too slow)
- Accountability
- Good organization
- No wasted practice time: working hard and smart

Play Hard (Have Fun)

Playing hard is the opposite of working hard, but in football the two go hand in hand. The team that has fun—while still working hard in a highly disciplined manner—will bond. They will also have a sense of energy, excitement, and belief in the dream: winning championships. Having fun does not mean just joking around; it encompasses many factors including caring about the other guys on the team. And really being a team is one of the great gifts of this game. Football is the ultimate team sport. Having fun is thus composed of:

- Sense of humor
- Sense of camaraderie
- Enthusiasm
- Team loyalty
- Belief
- Inspiration
- Passion
- Excitement
- Teamwork
- Intensity
- Energy

Win Games

Winning games flows naturally from a disciplined, organized, extremely hardworking team whose players find joy and energy in working together and with the coaching staff. Of course, talent helps, as do good X's and O's! Remind your players of the lesson in the movie *Rudy*: work long enough and hard enough and never give up, and good things will happen. What better life skill can your players take away from football?

Appendices

APPENDIX A: RECEIVER TERMINOLOGY

Receiver Identification

In most offensive systems, receivers are referred to as letters of the alphabet. Typically:

- X = The receiver who is on the line of scrimmage and away from the tight end side of the formation: also called the wideout or split end.

- Z = The receiver who is typically on the same side of the formation as the tight end and usually aligns off the line. This position is also called the flanker.

- S = Inside (slot) receiver. Depending on the program, this receiver can also be denoted by letters such an A, T, H, or W. He is split out as the third or fourth receiver in a three- or four-receiver formation.

- Y = The tight end. The tight end may be attached to the formation in a three-point stance like a down lineman or flexed out away from the formation in a receiver's two-point stance.

Receiver Formations

Receivers (and other personnel) are grouped into different formations. Following are some common formations:

- *Pro formation* uses two wide receivers (X, Z), one tight end (Y), and two running backs. Pro left and pro right designate the side the tight end goes to (i.e., the strongside).

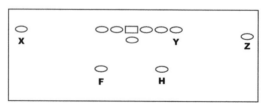

Figure A-1. Pro formation

- *Closed formation* uses no wide or slot receivers on one side of the formation. There will generally be a tight end on that side, one or two receivers on the other side of the formation, and two or three backs in the backfield.

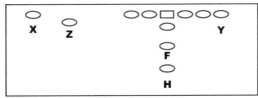

Figure A-2. Closed formation

- *Twins* means two receivers are on one side of the formation.

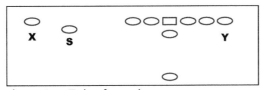

Figure A-3. Twins formation

- *Trips* means three receivers are to one side of the formation. The receivers can be aligned in various places depending on the program's philosophy.

Figure A-4. Trips formation

- *Doubles/2 x 2* means two receivers are on each side of the formation.

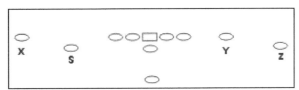

Figure A-5. Doubles formation

- *No backs* means no running backs are in the backfield. The most common version has three receivers to one side of the formation and two to the other.

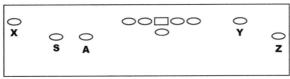

Figure A-6. No backs formation

- *Quads/4 x 1* has four receivers to one side and one receiver to the other. This look is somewhat trendy, but its longevity has yet to be tested.

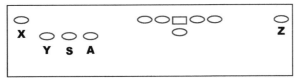

Figure A-7. Quads formation

APPENDIX B: RECEIVER WARM-UPS

This section provides a series of pre-game drills that are good to use for individual warm-up time before games. Following the drills are lists of useful activities for pre-practice during the season.

Pre-Game

Pre-game drills should include activities to:

- Get the receivers' legs warm.

- Get the receivers catching the football.

- Get the receivers involved in light contact. (Some pre-game contact is very important; do not let receivers go into a game "cold." It may take them a couple of plays to get into the hitting mode, and that's just wasted opportunity.)

- Build confidence. Despite the numerous pages of technique details reviewed in this book, so much of playing receiver is mental. Players must believe they can do it. Help your receivers get in the groove and improve confidence by using the same drills before every game (they like the familiarity and tradition). Pick drills they do well.

Getting Warm

Use some or all of these moving agilities from a correct stance in quick succession to get your receivers warmed up. All drills go 10 yards:

- Jog

- High knees (opens hips and groin)

- High knee crossover (opens hips)

- Butt kicks on tiptoes (opens groin and thighs)

- Carioca (works agility and quick feet, getting the torso and hips loose, and staying low)

- Backpedal (Yes, it's for defenders, but it works agility, staying on the balls of the feet, field awareness and balance, and most of all staying low—which, of course, is extremely important for receivers, too.)

Catching Drills

Warm-up catching drills (Chapter 2) are also excellent for pre-game warm-ups. They allow the receiver to get moving and catching without risking fatigue from running complete routes. These drills are crucial for reminding receivers (and their muscle memory) of catching techniques for the main kinds of passes:

- Coming across the field
- Ball thrown behind the receiver (flip the hips)
- Low ball
- High ball
- Fade

Also, run hitches and slants (time permitting). These short routes (again, no fatigue factor) work on two key types of breaks that are used in other routes. They have a high completion percentage when run on air and boost confidence before going into battle.

Release and Blocking Drills (Combined)

Have each receiver release on the line against a defender who jams him. He then runs 7 to 10 yards downfield, squares up on another defender, and stalk blocks him until the coach's signal. While this scenario might not occur often in games, it is a great drill for combining two key aspects of playing receiver. It also reminds the receivers in a concrete way that they must be *physical* to be successful.

Before Practice

Pre-Pre-Practice

This phase is truly before any part of practice has begun. Receivers have to run more than most players on the team, so they need to get dressed and out to the field very quickly and start getting loose. Pre-pre-practice activities may include:

- Individual stretching and jogging
- Receivers throwing the football back and forth to each other
- The quarterback (or coach) throwing easy balls to the receivers as they jog
- Bungee-ball work

Pre-Practice: Warm-Up Time

Official warm-up routines vary from school to school. In lieu of the entire team stretching together, sometimes you are allowed to warm-up your receivers as a group before practice has officially started, and you can use this time for:

- Static stretching (You may select a veteran receiver to lead this activity.)
- Moving agilities (see pre-game warm-up list)
- Discussing new plays

- Getting to know your players better as people
- Working on plants (cone drills), releases, and blocking techniques, because individual receiver practice periods may be very limited (especially later in the season)

General Comments on Drills

Whenever you can work on several things in one drill, do it. Repetition and good habits count for a lot in football. That is, work stance and takeoff all of the time. Whenever possible, even in release or break drills, throw a football to the receiver. Work the burst upfield after the catch routinely. Receivers have a lot to think about on the field during a game; give them a lot to think about during each drill. The more that becomes automatic the better.

As discussed, repetition (neuromuscular patterning) is key and therefore some drills need to be done on a daily basis—especially early in the season. However, keep it fresh by adding new drills that work on the same principles over the course of the season. Doing so will keep your practices exciting, and your players more alert, involved, and mentally stretched. Many drill books are available to add to the repertoire of basic drills in this book—or you can make up your own.

APPENDIX C: OFF-SEASON

Finger/Hand Exercises

Besides using classic V-shaped grippers and the Gripmaster hand-and-finger exercise (the best), some useful exercises to help improve hand-and-finger strength and awareness include:

- The receiver squeezes a tennis ball (or exercise putty ball).

- With one hand, the receiver picks up a sheet of spread-out newspaper off the floor and crumples it into a tighter and tighter ball. He squeezes that ball for a few seconds and then repeats the exercise with the other hand and another piece of newspaper. Next, he repeats this exercise by picking up two sheets of newspaper at one time, then three, and so on.

- The receiver grabs a handful of sand with his hand and attempts to mold it into a ball. He won't succeed, but it's a great exercise.

- The receivers partner up. One player holds the tip of the football in one hand. The other player grabs the other tip with one hand and tries to pull the football away. The players switch hands and do it again.

- Receivers can do various ball-handling drills. One simple drill is to have the receiver hold the ball in one hand, drop it, and try to catch it before it hits the ground. Another drill is for the receiver to handle the football with only one hand at a time and transfer the ball from one hand to another between his legs, behind his back, or around his head. Let the receivers be creative here and make up their own moves by playing on basketball's similar ball drills that the receivers are probably already familiar with. This chance to make up drills should add energy and enthusiasm to the exercise.

- Have the receivers play catch with a tennis ball to emphasize catching with their fingers. This drill also works hand-eye coordination. Another good idea is to put numbers on the ball and have the receivers call out the number as they catch the tennis ball. Doing so makes the receivers concentrate more.

Weights

Weight lifting is essential for an athlete—both in season and during the off-season as well. Most football programs have a designated strength and conditioning coach who will implement a program suitable for each position.

Basically, it is important that receivers have weight routines that work the entire body in order to maintain a proper equilibrium of strength within the body. Some kids will try to skip out on lifting for the lower body because they think that all of the running they do works this area enough. This belief is not true. In addition, special emphasis should be given to exercises that develop core strength to help with the explosion needed in blocking. Neck exercises are also important to strengthen the neck, which is vulnerable to serious injury in football.

Speed and Burst Work

It is extremely important for a receiver to maintain and even improve his form and technique as a sprinter. In fact, it would benefit the receiver corps as a whole to run track and field together in the off-season. Requisite speed and burst work includes drills made for sprinters:

- Stretches to achieve optimal flexibility by increasing muscle elasticity for sprinting. Static stretching or ballistic stretching (stretching with movement) may be use. Stretching also lessens the probability of injury.
- Plyometrics to improve speed, burst, and agility
- Sprints/running agilities, such as running 40-yard dashes or running through ropes

Please note that hundreds of drills can contribute to optimal speed and agility. This section only scratches the surface.

STATIC STRETCHES FOR THE LOWER BODY

Objective: To improve flexibility in the lower body

Descriptions:

- Hamstrings: The receiver sits on the ground with his legs out in front of him (or stands up) and reaches forward in an effort to touch his toes.
- Quads/Hip Flexors: While standing, the receiver grabs his right foot behind his body with his left hand and visa versa. (This approach is much better than using the same hand and foot to execute the stretch because there is less stress on the knee). Sinking the hips helps achieve an optimal stretch.
- Glutes: The receiver sits on the ground with one leg bent and over the other and hugs the knee of the bent leg to his opposite shoulder.
- Calves: The receiver leans forward with his hands on a wall and with his heels flat on the ground. He keeps moving his feet back until he gets to the spot where he feels the calves stretching.

BALLISTIC STRETCHING

Walking High Knees

Objective: To increase running motion flexibility

Description: The receiver walks in a straight line while lifting his knees as high as possible and hugging them to his chest. This exercise is a slow-moving drill.

Hurdle Step-Over

Objective: To increase running motion flexibility in the hips

Description: Set up six hurdles in one-yard intervals. The receiver walks along the right side of the hurdles while lifting his left knee and foot over the hurdles as he passes each one. The knee should clear the hurdle like the trail leg of a hurdler. He then goes back the other direction and uses his other leg.

RUNNING AGILITIES/SPRINTS

Running High Knees

Objective: To develop the muscle elasticity used in running

Description: This exercise is the traditional high-knee running motion. The height of the knee should be above parallel. The receiver works on the quickness of his knee action from the up position to the foot striking the ground. He should use vigorous arm movement, and good dorsa-flexion (i.e., the toes should be in an up position). The dorsa-flexion of the toes while running helps the foot to strike the ground with a quicker and more vigorous action.

Quick Skips

Objective: To develop muscle elasticity

Description: This drill is a fast skip while staying low to the ground (no jumping). Technique on the raised leg is similar to the high-knees exercise. The weight-bearing foot slides along the ground.

Butt Kicks

Objective: To promote elasticity and flexibility in the legs

Description: This exercise is a quick movement of the heel from the ground to the butt, with no lift in the knee, while running on the toes.

High-Knee Crossovers

Objective: To develop the muscle elasticity used in running with emphasis on the hip flexors

Description: For this traditional high-knee running motion with a crossover motion of the front leg, the receiver focuses on quickness of the knees from the up position to the foot striking the ground, the height of the knee (above parallel), vigorous arm movement, and the dorsa-flexion of the toes.

Bleachers or Hill Sprints

Objective: To develop overall muscles for the running motion, as well as to work on cardiovascular endurance

Description: The receiver starts from the bottom and runs up the bleachers or hill as quickly as possible while using correct running technique. The knee lift should be overexaggerated during this exercise to build the hip flexors (the muscles that lift the knees in the running motion).

PLYOMETRICS

Lunges

Objective: To develop muscles in the legs

Description: This regular walking lunge emphasizes arm movement and overall stability.

Lunge Hops

Objective: To develop fast-twitch muscles in the legs

Description: This drill is a lunge exercise with a hop in between. The receiver starts in a lunge position with his right leg forward and his left arm up. He then hops—working the fast-twitch muscles—to the next position of left foot forward and right arm up.

Bounding

Objective: To develop overall muscles for the running motion

Description: For this extra-long stride, the receiver hops from one leg to the other and pushes off aggressively while in a running motion.

Box Jumps

Objective: To enhance explosiveness in the leg muscles

Description: Several exercises include box jumps (jumping on top of the box and back down):

- Double-leg jumps from the front, and from each side of the box
- Double-leg jumps over the box from the front, and sideways from each side
- Single-leg jumps with each leg from the front, and sideways from each side
- Jumping over a series of boxes ranging from smaller to bigger

If no boxes are available, the receivers can jump in squares taped on the floor in the same succession.

Yoga and Pilates

The use of yoga and Pilates instruction for football players is becoming more common, and is not without historical precedence. The Green Bay Packers of the National Football League held ballet classes for their players as early as the 1960s in order for them to gain some of the benefits yoga and Pilates provide.

YOGA

Yoga, like ballet, increases flexibility, balance, concentration, and core strength. NFL running back Eddie George was one of the early and vocal proponents of yoga. More and more pro football players—from Shannon Sharpe of the Denver Broncos to Dan Marino of the Miami Dolphins—joined George in espousing the benefits of yoga.

Football programs at all levels of the game have begun incorporating yoga into their regular fitness programs. Yoga is a fixture in the workout programs at some high schools. For example, Nolan Catholic High School, Fort Worth, Texas (2004 TAPPS 5A state champions), began incorporating yoga in their football program in 2001. They credit it with giving their players greater flexibility and reducing significantly the number of injuries their players suffer. In fact, they have had only one muscle injury since yoga was incorporated as the third component of their weight and conditioning program. At higher levels of the game, college and NFL teams have joined the yoga bandwagon as well, making it an official part of their programs. The Tennessee Titans, for example, began team yoga classes in 2002 after they saw the results Eddie George was getting.

Why Yoga for Football?

- Stretching—Stretches are important before and after strenuous activity. Stretching is a key component of yoga. Yoga not only incorporates deep stretching, but also teaches players how to work through and reach a point in their stretches of maximum tension, which ultimately leads to greater relaxation of the muscle. It thus helps eliminate a lot of "fake" stretching that athletes at lower levels tend to engage in. Also, the stretching aspects of yoga help reduce stiffness—especially when used as a next-day follow-up to a game or a very intense workout or practice.

- Strength and Stability—Due to its emphasis on lengthening muscles, yoga makes a great counterpoint to weightlifting. It works the same muscles as weights do, but *lengthens* those muscles while lifting bulks them up. Athletes thus end up with more power, along with improved stability, agility, and flexibility.

- Balance/Control—Yoga involves a lot of work with stabilizer muscles, which tend to be neglected in most other types of workouts. These muscles aide in balance and body control—two elements that are especially important for receivers.

- Concentration—Yoga builds concentration. This skill is useful for all players, but receivers may benefit the most since loss of concentration is one of the key reasons for dropped passes.

- Flexibility—Yoga increases flexibility, which improves range of motion in a particular joint, and that means more wide-ranging power. Additionally, increased flexibility/mobility in a particular area (shoulders/hips) may make a player more elusive by helping them juke more effectively. Players may also be more able to survive being contorted in weird positions under a pile.

- Reduced Number of Injuries—The greater flexibility, as well as better overall body alignment, achieved through yoga means fewer injuries for your players and possibly longer careers for them. From the high school level to the pro level, a reduced number of injuries is one of the main benefits of yoga.

- Improvement in Chronic Injuries—For players nursing chronic injuries, yoga reduces pain and stiffness, and promotes healing by stretching muscles and increasing circulation in the affected area. Additionally, by improving overall body alignment, yoga may prevent compensating injuries, which occur when the body becomes misaligned in an attempt to compensate for an injured muscle or joint.

- Muscle Endurance—The more intense postures in yoga build strength by increasing muscle endurance. This complements weight-lifting programs designed to concentrate on brute strength and overall power.

- Cardiovascular Benefits—Only a couple of types of yoga might be technically considered cardiovascular exercises (power yoga, for example). However, through breathing exercises, all types of yoga provide some benefits similar to a cardio workout including:

  ○ Increased lung capacity and oxygen intake.

  ○ Improved oxygen exchange.

- Mental Focus—The emphasis on breathing, focus/concentration work, and even the relaxation aspects of yoga sharpen a player's mental abilities, as well as his physical abilities.

PILATES

Pilates is a form of exercise developed in the early 1900s. It is designed to increase flexibility and improve balance and coordination by strengthening the body's core or midsection. Pilates is used by professional-level athletes in many sports, including golf, basketball, baseball, and football.

Pilates is one of the fastest-growing fitness activities in the United States and is rapidly growing in popularity in the football world, as well. Specifically, Pilates is beneficial for football because it promotes more efficient movement, increased endurance and speed, and better agility and quickness. It builds the leg and glute muscles, which are essential for running, kicking, and making quick, effective cuts. Because Pilates trains the core (abdominal muscles and spine), it is useful in all aspects of football, but especially in blocking and tackling. A routine practice of Pilates can help to prevent injuries and reduce recovery time from injuries.

Several NFL teams, including the Buffalo Bills, the Detroit Lions, the Oakland Raiders, and the Tampa Bay Buccaneers, have incorporated Pilates into their regular workout regimen. At the college level, the 2005 National Champion University of Texas Longhorns football team has an assistant strength coach who conducts regular Pilates training with the football team. A 2004 article in the *Boston Herald* stated that the "oddity of football players participating in yoga, Pilates, and other unconventional training methods has long ago dissipated."

In a 2003 *USA Today* article, Chicago Bears Pro Bowl offensive guard Ruben Brown enthusiastically summed up the football-related benefits of Pilates: "I came out of the season injury-free," he says. "I used to feel like crap after practice and games, but not since Pilates. I learned how to breathe through my muscles. My posture is better. I can run more fluidly. And I increased my bench workouts."

APPENDIX D: FILM STUDY AND TESTS

Two types of receiver tests are included as samples in this section. The first test, for use in middle school, reviews basic receiver concepts and terminology. The second test is based on film review of the upcoming opponent and is appropriate for high school or college programs.

Middle School Wide Receiver's Test

1. At what depth do we break the stop route? _____

2. What is a corner route? Where do we break? _____

3. Name three routes where we make our break at the same depth. What depth is it?
   _____

4. When do we break on the slant route? _____

5. On our passing tree, odd numbered routes are run to the inside. True or false? (Circle one.)

6. Bonus Question: What is a PCP route? _____
   _____

7. How do you define splashdown? _____
   _____

8. What does *cushion* mean? _____
   _____

9. The main kind of block we use is a _____ block.

10. Who runs on the field when the coach shouts: "Ace, Trio, Regular, Rocket"?
    _____

11. Every time you catch a football in practice, what are you supposed to shout?
    _____

12. Coverages 2, 3, and 4 are man or zone? (Circle one.)

13. In cover 2, how many defenders are responsible for the deep part of the field? How many are responsible for the underneath part? _____

14. Name two ways to tell if it is man or zone coverage. _____

_____

15. How can you tell if it is cover 2 versus cover 3? _____

_____

16. Name one route that would be successful to run against cover 4. _____

_____

17. Trips and trey both mean there are _____ (how many) receivers on one side of the formation.

18. In formations, which player tells us which side the strongside is? What is the letter we call that player? _____

High School/College Film Study Quiz

Name _____ Team Viewed _____

Date _____ Tape Viewed _____

Myself

1. I must be especially alert for the following this week: _____

_____

2. I must improve my game this week by: _____

_____

3. One thing to focus on in particular each day in practice:

Monday _____

Tuesday _____

Wednesday _____

Thursday _____

4. My goals for this week are: _____

My Opponent

1. Player identification

Left corners' numbers   _____ _____

Right corners' numbers   _____ _____

Safeties' numbers   _____ _____

Linebackers' numbers   _____ _____

Nickel backs' numbers   _____ _____

Do they play "corners over"? Yes   No

Who is the best cornerback? Number _____ Name _____

How can you beat him? _____

Do they run with motion or bump over? _____

2.   Strengths   Weaknesses

Left cornerback _____

_____

Right cornerback _____

_____

Safety _____

_____

Linebacker _____

_____

Nickel _____

_____

3. What is their base coverage? In what situations do they get out of their base coverage? _____

4. Do they disguise their coverages or show them? If they disguise, what are the two disguises they use the most often from which to shift to their base coverage? ___

_____

5. Do they press? _____

6. What coverages are they in when they press?_____

_____

7. Do the corners bump-and-run in man? Or do they play soft man? _____

_____

8. What is their goal-line coverage and techniques? _____

_____

9. What coverage(s) do you expect in third-and-long? _____

_____

10. What blitzes do they use? _____

_____

11. How does "your" cornerback defeat the stalk block? _____

_____

APPENDIX E: GRADING SHEETS

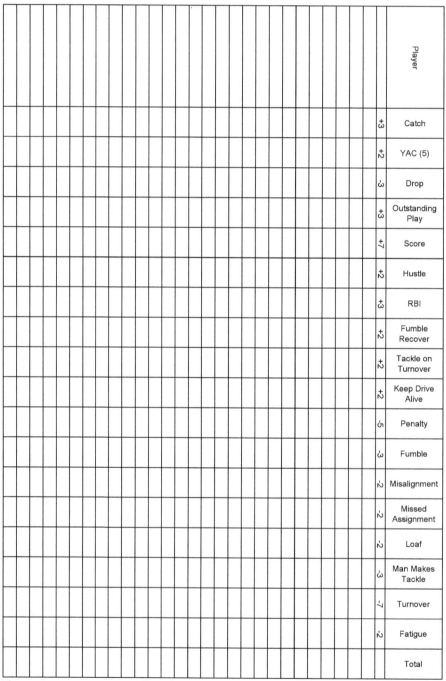

	Player
+3	Catch
+2	YAC (5)
-3	Drop
+3	Outstanding Play
+7	Score
+2	Hustle
+3	RBI
+2	Fumble Recover
+2	Tackle on Turnover
+2	Keep Drive Alive
-5	Penalty
-3	Fumble
-2	Misalignment
-2	Missed Assignment
-2	Loaf
-3	Man Makes Tackle
-7	Turnover
-2	Fatigue
	Total

Figure E-1. Post-game grading sheet

STAY STUCK POLICE - BLOCKING CRIMES			
Player #	Name	Play	Blocking Error

Figure E-2. Stay Stuck Police: blocking crimes

APPENDIX F: LEGEND

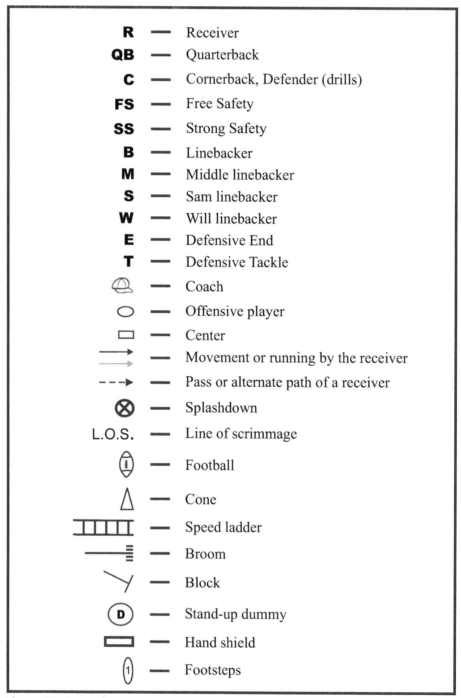

R	—	Receiver
QB	—	Quarterback
C	—	Cornerback, Defender (drills)
FS	—	Free Safety
SS	—	Strong Safety
B	—	Linebacker
M	—	Middle linebacker
S	—	Sam linebacker
W	—	Will linebacker
E	—	Defensive End
T	—	Defensive Tackle
	—	Coach
	—	Offensive player
	—	Center
	—	Movement or running by the receiver
	—	Pass or alternate path of a receiver
	—	Splashdown
L.O.S.	—	Line of scrimmage
	—	Football
	—	Cone
	—	Speed ladder
	—	Broom
	—	Block
	—	Stand-up dummy
	—	Hand shield
	—	Footsteps

Figure F-1. Legend

Alignment: The location of the receiver on the field before the snap in relationship to the sideline and the offensive line.

Alley: Part of the field between the numbers and the box.

Audible: Verbal commands from the quarterback to his teammates by which he changes the play at the line of scrimmage just prior to the snap.

Backfield: The area behind the line of scrimmage where the quarterback and running backs are located.

Backs: The running backs (fullback, halfback, tailback, wing back).

Backside: Side of the formation or field where the play is not going.

Bail: When the defender backpedals before, at, or after the snap.

Banjo: When two defenders switch responsibilities while covering two offensive players.

Blitz: When a defender who does not normally rush pursues the quarterback.

Blocking: Preventing a defender from getting to the ballcarrier.

Bootleg: The quarterback fakes a handoff to a running back on one side and rolls out to the other side of the field. Normally, receivers run routes in the direction in which the quarterback is rolling.

Box: Area from tackle to tackle.

Bump-and-Run: A technique used by a defender in press coverage in which he attempts to make contact with the receiver within five yards of the line of scrimmage to disrupt the route. The defender then follows the receiver wherever he goes on the field to prevent a completion.

Bunch: Formation in which all receivers are aligned closely together (usually one yard apart).

Carioca: Warm-up drill that involves crossing over the legs to loosen the hips.

Clipping: Blocking an opponent below the waist from behind.

Corners Over: When the cornerback goes to the other side of the field for coverage if no receivers are on his side of the formation.

Coverage: 1. The attempt of a defender to prevent a player from gaining yards; in pass coverage a defender prevents the receiver from catching a pass. 2. A defensive system designed to prevent the offense from gaining yards.

Crack Block: When a receiver goes inside to block a linebacker or safety.

Cushion: The distance, pre-snap and during the route, between the receiver and the defender.

Cut Block: Legally blocking an opponent below the waist from the front.

Glossary

Drift: To stray, either upfield, downfield, or sideways, off the intended path.

False Stepping: Any extra foot movement that does not directly aid in takeoff.

First Level: Term used to describe the area from the line of scrimmage to the point where the linebackers are covering during a play (generally, 10 yards from the line of scrimmage).

Flanker: The receiver who aligns off the line of scrimmage prior to the snap. This receiver is often on the same side of the formation as the tight end.

Flat: 1. Area of the field from the end of the box to the sideline, and from the line of scrimmage up to 10 yards deep. 2. A route to this area of the field.

Flexed: When the tight end is lined up as a slot or wide receiver.

Foot-Fire: Rapid up-and-down foot movement on the balls of the feet while the player is running in place.

High Point It: Jumping to catch the ball at the highest point possible.

Holding: A penalty that results when a player illegally grabs or hooks any part of his opponent's body or uniform. It usually becomes apparent when the jersey gets pulled away from the defender's body or a part of the body is grasped.

Hot: Term for a receiver that is uncovered or is about to become uncovered because the defender covering him is blitzing.

Invert: A defensive term used for switching responsibilities between two players.

Leverage: Alignment on the inside, head-up, or the outside of an opponent to create a favorable position.

Motion: Movement (never forward) behind the line of scrimmage by a receiver or running back before or while the ball is snapped.

Neutral Zone: 1. The area equal to the length of the ball as it sits on the ground before each play. 2. The area between the two lines of scrimmage (offensive and defensive).

Off The Line (Off the Ball): Alignment of an offensive player who is not on the line of scrimmage. Off-the-ball receivers are usually one yard behind the line of scrimmage.

Offside: A penalty that occurs when any part of a player's body is over the line of scrimmage when the ball is snapped.

On The Line (On the Ball): Alignment of offensive players such as the linemen, tight end, and split end on the line of scrimmage. Seven offensive players must be on the line.

Option Plays: An offensive play in which the quarterback has the choice (option) of handing or pitching the ball to a running back, running the ball himself, or, in some systems, passing the football.

Overpursue: To go beyond the optimal point to make contact with an opponent usually caused by taking a poor angle. A missed tackle or missed block results because his running momentum makes the player unable to recover from the bad angle.

Passing Tree: A diagram of all of the passing routes for a particular offense.

Playside: Side of the formation and field where the play is going.

Pocket: The area behind and inside the offensive linemen where the quarterback is protected by his blockers from rushing defenders.

Power Center: Area of the body from the stomach to the thighs where balance, strength, and explosion come from.

Pre-Snap Read: Determining what the defensive coverage is before the ball is snapped.

Press Man: Playing man-to-man defense with the intent of making contact with the receiver as he releases off the line of scrimmage to disrupt the route being run.

Quads: Four receivers to one side of an offensive formation.

RAC: Run after the catch (a.k.a. YAC, yards after the catch).

Read: Determining what the opponent has planned and/or is executing.

Red Zone: Area on each side of the field from the goal line to the 20-yard line where the offense is driving to score.

Release: Path and technique that a receiver uses to go from the line of scrimmage into the route being run.

Riverside: Reversing sides or switching directions.

Roll Out: When the quarterback runs outside of the pocket to the left or right to execute a pass play designed to go to that side. Normally receivers run routes in the direction in which the quarterback is rolling.

Second Level: Term used to describe the area from the linebackers to the deep defenders during a play (generally, from 10 to 20 yards from the line of scrimmage).

Shift: The movement of more than one offensive or defensive player before the snap. These players must come to a stop and be set for at least one second before the snap.

Slot: Receiver aligned in the area of the field between the tackle (or tight end) and the wide receiver. Usually, he is aligned off the ball.

Splashdown: Where the ball is expected to be caught.

Splits (Narrow) (Wide): For a receiver, this term means how far removed from the end man on the line (tackle/tight end) he is prior to the snap. Narrow splits means the receiver is closer to that lineman, and wide splits means the receiver is closer to the sideline.

Stalk Block: Upright block a receiver uses to prevent a defender from making a play on the ballcarrier.

Stem: Initial part of a receiver's pass route from his alignment at the line of scrimmage to the breakpoint.

Stick: 1. A plant step made by a receiver. 2. Hard throw (on a line) by the quarterback.

Stretch: Outside running play (off tackle) to the alley in which the running back receives the ball through a handoff.

Strongside: Generally, the side of an offensive formation where the tight end aligns (can also be called the strength).

Swap Hips: When a receiver brings his hips parallel to, or ahead of, those of the defender to complete his release move.

Sweep: Outside run play (off tackle) by the running back in which the ball is tossed instead of handed off.

Third Level: Term used to describe the area of the field covered by the deep defenders during a play (generally, 20-plus yards).

To The Boundary: When the ball is placed on a hash mark, it is the side of the field that is closest to that sideline. That is, when the ball is placed on the left hash, it is the left side of the field from the hash marks to the sideline.

To The Field: When the ball is placed on a hash mark, it is the side of the field that is farther away from that sideline. That is, when the ball is placed on the left hash, it is the right side of the field from the left hash marks to the right sideline.

Toe Drag: A move made by the receiver to keep the toes inbounds while reaching out and catching a ball thrown on or over the sideline or edge of the end zone.

Trail Technique: When the defensive player lets the receiver by and follows him up the field.

Trey: Formation with three receivers to one side, usually including a tight end.

Trips: Formation with three receivers to one side.

Uncovered: A receiver who does not have a defender lined up on him.

Underneath: The area from the quarterback to the point where linebackers are during a play (first level).

Window: 1. Frame formed by the receiver's hands that he looks through while making a catch. 2. A void in the coverage. 3. An unobstructed view of the receiver by the quarterback (a.k.a. passing lane).

YAC: Yards after the catch (a.k.a. RAC, run after the catch).

S. Chuck Myers is the tight ends coach at Paul Quinn College in Dallas, Texas. Previously, Myers served as head football coach at St. Vincent's Episcopal School in Bedford, Texas, where Myers designed and implemented the school's first middle and high school football programs. In 2003, as the tight ends coach at Bishop Lynch High School in Dallas, Texas, Myers helped lead the team to the Texas TAPPS 5A state championship. However, Myers is best known as a wide receivers coach, having coached at several Dallas-area high schools, including Covenant Christian Academy (Colleyville), Fort Worth Country Day School (Fort Worth), and The Oakridge School (Arlington).

Myers enjoys giving back to the community by coaching at programs designed for inner-city youth. Myers has served as a head coach in the NFL's Junior Player Development program, and has coached at a number of Play It Smart camps and similar camps on the East Coast, as well as in Texas.

Acknowledged as a technician and a true student of the game, Myers has spent the last decade gaining knowledge of the receiver position by spending significant time at a wide range of football programs. These include Southlake (TX) Carroll High School (the 2002, 2004, and 2005 Texas state champions and the 2004 and 2005 Mythical National Champions), the University of North Texas, and Southern Methodist University.

Myers has an MBA from Harvard Business School and previously worked as an investment banker on Wall Street and in Europe. After growing up in Kansas City and living in Boston, New York, Germany, and England, Myers moved to Texas in 1992 and, like most residents of the state, became a football addict.

My then seven-year-old daughter wanted to "help" me write this book one night. (By the way, for those of you who are thinking of writing a book, she is now 10.) The following is what she scribbled. I think it sums up pretty well how I feel about this game.

Postscript

The Authors Page

I have loved football for all of my life but I have always been kind, hearted to others. I belive it's important to win but also to just have fun. I think footbal is a good sport because it enhasis ze skills more then any thing else!